Lecture Notes in Computer S

Edited by G. Goos and J. Hartmanis

A. Cheese

Parallel Execution of Parlog

Springer-Verlag
Berlin Heidelberg New York
London Paris Tokyo
Hong Kong Barcelona
Budapest

Series Editors

Gerhard Goos
Universität Karlsruhe
Postfach 69 80
Vincenz-Priessnitz-Straße 1
W-7500 Karlsruhe, FRG

Juris Hartmanis
Department of Computer Science
Cornell University
5149 Upson Hall
Ithaca, NY 14853, USA

Author

Andrew Cheese
Siemens-Nixdorf Information Systems AG, Multiprocessor Unix Kernel Group
Otto Hahn Ring 6, W-8000 Munich 83, FRG

CR Subject Classification (1991): D.3.4

ISBN 3-540-55382-7 Springer-Verlag Berlin Heidelberg New York
ISBN 0-387-55382-7 Springer-Verlag New York Berlin Heidelberg

Typesetting: Camera ready by author
Printing and binding: Druckhaus Beltz, Hemsbach/Bergstr.
45/3140-543210 - Printed on acid-free paper

·eface

gic programming has been proposed as a programming methodology that may help in producing re reliable and maintainable computing systems than those presently in service. At the same time re has been a trend for making faster computers by building machines using multiple CPUs. As a ult of these two factors a family of concurrent logic languages has been developed to tackle the blems of programming these parallel computer architectures. It is important that the plementations of such computer languages should be efficient, otherwise the benefits of allelism will be lost.

is monograph concentrates on the programming language Parlog and on computational models its efficient execution. Two such models are developed, one a fine-grain Packet-Rewriting del and the other more coarse-grained, the Multi-Sequential model. Both models are reviewed in ail and software simulators have been built for them. Results from the simulations show that the lti-Sequential model is very promising whereas the Packet-Rewriting model does not appear to table for the efficient execution of logic languages. These results have considerable importance the design of parallel logic programming systems, and the implications are outlined and cussed in the concluding chapter.

ave many people to thank for helping me with this research. First and most of all, I would like to nk my supervisor, David Brailsford for all his help and encouragement during my research.

n very grateful to the following people for proof-reading sections, and in some cases all, of this nograph and for their comments : Uri Baron, Steve Benford, David Brailsford, Mark O'Brien, gio Delgado-Rannauro, Dave Elliman, Colin Higgins, Graem Ringwood, Andy Walker, and rion Windsor.

rion Windsor, the secretary of the Department of Computer Science, University of Nottingham, ; particularly helpful throughout the course of this research.

I would like to thank the following members of the Department of Computing Science at th University of Nottingham for providing a friendly and stimulating working environment, Willia Armitage, Peter Cowan, David Evans, David Ford, Eric Foxley, Godwin Gwei, Leon Harriso Mike Heard, Roger Henry, Phillipa Hennessey, Emiko Hiraga, Kevin Hopkins, Anne Loma Graeme Lunt, Julian Onions, William Shu, Hugh Smith, and Mary Tolley.

Special thanks are due to Simone Mahlenbrei who helped me at various times whilst I was puttin the finishing touches to this book at the European Computer-Industry Research Centre Gmb (ECRC).

This research was funded by the UK Science and Engineering Research Council (SERC).

February 1992 Andrew Chees

›ntents

ıapter 1 Introduction

ckground 1
gic Programming 4
velopments in Prolog Implementation 9
mputer Architecture Developments 12
·allelism in Logic Programs 12
ncurrent Logic Programming 14
jectives and Contributions of this Research 24
›view of Book Contents 25

ıapter 2 Parlog A Concurrent Logic Programming Language

roduction 27
ncurrency 27
er-Process Communication 27
leterminacy 29
ıchronization 30
ıer Parlog Syntax and Operational Features 31
ample Programs 33
mpilation 35
osen Dialect 45

ıapter 3 A Fine-Grain Graph Reduction Model of Computation

roduction 48
ıph Reduction 49
e Computational Model 51
ture of Packets 52

Packet Structure
Operational Semantics of the Model
Sharing of Computation
Packet Description Language
An Example
Selectors and Constructors
Remarks on the Model of Computation

Chapter 4 Implementing Parlog on a Packet-Rewriting Computational Model

Introduction
The Implementation
Throttling
Evaluation
Summary

Chapter 5 The Multi-Sequential Coarse-Grain Approach

Multi-Sequential Architectures
Code Space
Data Space
Processing Element Structure
Environments
Task Data Structures
Control Data Structures
Management of Queue Data Structures
Load Balancing

covery from Resource Exhaustion 111
stract Instruction Set 112
nulation of Model 120
mmary 132

apter 6 Summary, Further Work and Conclusions

roduction 133
e Packet-Rewriting Model 133
e Multi-Sequential Model 136
mparison of the Packet-Rewriting and Multi-Sequential Models 138
rther Work 140
nclusions 144

pendix 1 Fine-Grain Execution of merge/3 147

pendix 2 A Physical Bit-Level Packet Representation 157

pendix 3 PPM Instruction Set Listing 159

pendix 4 Compiled Form of merge/3 for PPM 161

bliography 165

Chapter 1 Introduction

Background

There is a growing recognition that there is a "software crisis" [3] in the sense that software systems are becoming too complex for the available programming languages and tools to handle. There are numerous computer-related disasters which lead one to believe that this is true [105]. These include reports of many Space Shuttle launch failures because of faulty software, the Vancouver Stock Index losing 574 points over 22 months as a result of a software rounding error, an *F18* aircraft crashing because of a missing exception condition, and *Viking* having a misaligned antenna caused by a faulty code patch.

The range of widely used imperative programming languages and the bad programming styles they tend to encourage are frequently cited as a major cause of faulty software. The meaning of the adjective "imperative" is "commanding". In fact, more often than not, the only means of understanding an imperative language program is as an ordered set of state-changing commands. This is because imperative programming languages are based on the von-Neumann model of computation, whereby a processing element is tightly-coupled with memory and executes a series of instructions guided by a program counter which indicates the "next instruction" to be obeyed. The notion of global memory is inherent in such programming language designs and together with the use of destructive assignment of new information to be stored can cause unforseen side-effects leading to obscure program bugs. An example of this might occur when a global and local variable differ by one character in their names and the global name is used by mistake for the local name. This error would remain undetected because the destructive-assignment statement is syntactically and semantically correct. In short, the solving of a problem with an imperative programming language requires not only a specification of *what* the solution is, but also a description of *how* to solve the problem.

The answer seems to lie in a paradigm which allows the programmer to state, declaratively, a description of a solution to the problem at hand and lets the target machinery perform the necessary computation. This philosophy has encouraged computer programmers to look towards the descriptive formalism of mathematical logic to help them achieve this goal. The result is a family of so-called declarative languages. In fact there are two camps of declarative programmers who support either the logic programming or the functional programming style. There are fundamental differences in these two styles [44] but in both cases the resulting program consists of a set of assertive equations and computation is the deduction of some property with respect to these assertions.

Declarative language programs can be understood by static analysis because the meaning of any individual program segment is independent of the meaning of all the other textually separate parts. This, in turn, means that the semantics of the entire program is independent of the order of evaluation of these parts [97]. Therefore it is perfectly safe to evaluate declarative programs using a parallel computational model. All parallelism is implicit in the program, implying that the degree of concurrency exploitable is limited only by the degree of inherent parallelism present in the program.

Functional programming languages are directional; that is, the inputs and outputs of the relations they define are statically determined. As a result they utilise one-way pattern matching as a parameter passing mechanism. This is a drawback compared to the lack of modality (nonspecification of whether arguments are inputs or outputs) which is inherent in the logic programming paradigm. In the conventional imperative programming sense of parameter passing, this means that arguments can be used as either inputs or outputs, the correct mode being determined at runtime by the logic programming system and not by the user. An example of this property is the `append/3` (the notation `f/n` meaning `f` is a symbol of a structure of `n` arguments) relation allowing the user to specify a program which can be used both to concatenate two lists and to split a list into two sublists.

The functional paradigm does enable very powerful and flexible data type systems to be developed [16], allowing the user to define arbitrary types. The declarative and operational semantics of a functional programming language are based upon the lambda calculus [5] [25], and a reduction model of computation [172], respectively. A functional programmer will think in terms of functions and their evaluation. The most widely used of functional programming languages is the functional subset of Lisp [182]. However, there are now more powerful programming languages based on the lambda-calculus such as Miranda [167], SML [76] [55], and Haskell [171].

Logic programming languages are relational; a program is a conjunction of equations each expressing a relation between objects of interest to the programmer. Each equation is an implication stating that a property of an object or properties of a set of objects, are conditional on other object properties being true. In order to determine whether properties are true or false it is usual for the programmer to express some relations between objects that are vacuously true. Each equation is called a "clause" and a set of ordered clauses having the same relation name, "predicate symbol", is called a "relation" or "procedure".

Logic programming systems employ "unification" as a parameter-passing mechanism. As an example consider unifying the head of a clause `p(X, 2, Z)` with a goal `p(1, Y, 3)`, where a goal is analagous to a procedure call in conventional imperative programming languages with two-way parameter passing, and variables are denoted by lexical items beginning with a capital letter. The unification procedure is concerned with finding substitutions of variables to make a set of terms equal. In the example the substitution would be `{ X/1, Y/2, Z/3 }`, where the notation `V/t` denotes that the variable `V` is bound to the term `t`. Unlike the case of executing functional programming languages, it is possible to bind variables in the goal, e.g. `Y` in the above example. This enables logic programmers to make use of so-called "logical variables", that is, they are allowed to instantiate variables to terms which are non-ground i.e. the terms contain variables. For instance, consider the term `request(S)`. The variable `S` can be bound to another term `message(info, Answer)` which itself contains the variable `Answer`. This powerful feature enables a relation to only deal with the part of a data structure it is interested in, leaving "holes" to be filled in by other, more appropriate, relations. A practical use of this is in building one-pass compilers. Conventionally compilers written in imperative programming languages are two-pass. The first pass simply gathers up all the symbols in a program and makes a note of where they are in the program, so that on the second pass these symbol references can be filled in correctly. If the compiler is written in a logic programming language it suffices to leave the reference to the symbol as a variable which can be instantiated to the correct address later, when this has been determined. The procedural and declarative semantics of logic programming languages have foundations in theorem proving and predicate logic [99].

The declarative programming language paradigm has now been recognised as a viable alternative to conventional imperative approaches. As a result of this, several industrial organisations are now embarking on research programmes focusing on logic programming. Examples of these are the European Computer-Industry Research Centre (ECRC) in Munich, West Germany, funded jointly by Bull SA, Siemens and ICL [151] [54]; the Software Technology Division at MCC in Texas, U.S.A.; the Institute of New Generation Computer Technology (ICOT) which, although funded by the Japanese government, most of the researchers are from industry [63]; and the Swedish Institute of Computer Science (SICS) [176], which has been formed using 50% funding from the Swedish government but with help from industry. There is still a long way to go, however, before research results will reach the bulk of computer product consumers and until that time the majority of computer users may remain unconvinced of logic programming's potential.

Logic Programming

The state of logic programming is now arguably more advanced than that of the functional paradigm. This can be traced to the spread of Prolog, both in academic circles and industry [122] [123] [124] [125]. Logic programming language systems are more usable than their functional programming counterparts. Quintus Prolog for instance, provides a very good development environment incorporating modules, type-checking and other tools [121].

Theoretical Background

In order to describe the logic programming paradigm, it is necessary to review both the syntax and semantics of first-order predicate logic. Syntactically, first-order predicate logic is defined by a language over some alphabet. This alphabet consists of variables, constants, functions, predicates, connectives, quantifiers and punctuation symbols. The last three classes of symbols are the same for any formula of the logic. The connectives are $\sim$, $\wedge$, $\vee$, $\rightarrow$ and $\leftrightarrow$. Their intended meanings are "negation", "conjunction", "disjunction", "implication" and "equivalence". The quantifiers are represented by the symbols $\forall$, meaning universal quantification i.e. "for all", and $\exists$ meaning existential quantification i.e. "there exists". The punctuation symbols are "(", ")" and ",". Variables are normally represented by capital letters, e.g. X, Y, and Z. Constants are represented by letters near the start of the Roman alphabet such as a, b and c. Function symbols are denoted by letters chosen from a third of the way through the Roman alphabet such as f, g, and h. Predicate symbols are denoted by letters chosen from two-thirds of the way through the Roman alphabet, e.g. p, q, and r.

The terms of first-order predicate logic are defined inductively. All variables are terms, all constants are terms, and if f is a function (or functor) of arity n and t1, ..., tn are terms then f(t1, ..., tn) is a term. The well-formed formulas of first-order predicate logic are also defined inductively. If p is a predicate symbol of arity n and t1, ..., tn are terms, then p(t1, ..., tn) is a formula. In this specific case the formula is called an "atom" (in the logic programming world, as opposed to theoretical logic studies, atom also refers to a constant). If F and G are formulas then so are ~F, F ∧ G, F ∨ G, F → G, and F ↔ G. If F is a formula and X is a variable then ∀X F and ∃X F are formulas.

In the quantified formulas ∀X F and ∃X F the variable X is said to be "bound". In general, all occurrences of a variable following a quantifier which are also present in the quantified formula are "bound". Any variable present in a formula which is not bound is said to be "free". For instance, in the formula ∀X p(X, Y), X is bound and Y is free. A formula with no free occurrences of variables is said to be "closed".

A "literal" is an atom or the negation of an atom. A "positive literal" is simply an atom and a "negative literal" is the negation of an atom. A "clause" is a closed universally quantified disjunction of literals. That is, it is of the form

∀X1 ... ∀Xn (L1 ∨ ... ∨ Lm)

where each Li is a literal and each Xi is a variable. Logic programs consist of a set of clauses. Thus a special notation can be adopted to make programs easier to read. The clause

∀X1 ... ∀Xn (A1 ∨ ... ∨ Aj ∨ ~B1 ∨ ... ∨ ~Bk)

can be represented in this new semantically equivalent clausal form notation as

A1, ..., Aj ← B1, ..., Bk

where all the variables, X1, ..., Xn, are assumed to be universally quantified. The commas in the consequent, A1, ..., Aj, denote disjunction and the commas in the consequent, B1, ..., Bk, denote conjunction.

A "program clause" is a clause containing exactly one positive literal and takes the form A ← B1, ..., Bk. A is called the "head" and B1, ..., Bk the "body" of the program clause. A "unit clause" is a program clause with an empty body, that is, it takes the form A ←. The informal meaning of a program clause such as A ← B1, ..., Bk is that if for every assignment of each variable in the above clause, the conjuncts B1, ..., Bk are true then A is true. Program clauses with non-empty bodies are "conditional" and unit clauses, with empty bodies, are "unconditional". The informal intended meaning of the unit clause A ← is that, for each assignment of each variable in the clause, the literal A is true. A "goal clause" contains no positive literals and is of the form ← B1, ..., Bk. Each Bi is called a "subgoal" of the clause. The "empty clause", with no antecedent or consequent, is understood as meaning a contradiction. A "Horn clause" is either a program clause or a goal clause, that is, there is at most one positive literal present.

Most logic programming language dialects are based upon the Horn clause subset of first-order predicate logic. One of the properties of first-order predicate logic is that it has equivalent operational and declarative semantics. The procedural meaning of a theory is given by a "proof theory", that is, it is a corresponding "proof tree". A proof may proceed by negating the formula that is to be proved and trying to obtain a contradiction using the clauses making up the program, thus concluding that the original unnegated formula is a logical consequence of the program.

A proof may use use of a procedure known as "resolution" to construct its derivation. A logic programming system makes use of resolution to try and reduce the given query (a goal clause, in fact the negation of what is actually to be proved) to the empty clause. It does this by first selecting a literal from the goal clause and attempting to unify it with the head of a program clause. If this succeeds the original literal is replaced by all the body literals giving a new goal clause. The unifying substitution is then applied to this new clause and the whole process reiterates. If the attempted unification should fail, the system will attempt to select a literal again. This chosen literal could be the same one again, in which case an alternative clause for the predicate would be used, and unification attempted. This whole process repeats until the empty clause is derived or until it is discovered that there is no route available for the computation to proceed and it would then be concluded that the original goal clause is not a logical consequence of the program. The current goal clause is called the "resolvant".

Consider the effect of resolution on the goal clause and program clauses given below.

```
← p(X, 1), q(X, Y).
```

```
p(2, Z).
q(1, 1).
q(2, 2).
```

The first thing the resolution process does is to select an atom from the current goal clause. In the programming language Prolog the leftmost atom is chosen. Assume then that this is the "selection function" used, meaning that the atom `p(X, 1)` is selected. This unifies with the first program clause giving a substitution `{X/2, Z/1}` which means that the variables `X` and `Z` are bound to the constants `2` and `1`. Applying this substitution to the current goal gives us a new resolvant `q(2, Y)`. There are two program clauses defining the procedure `q/2`. Unification of the current goal with the first of them fails because the constants `1` and `2` are unequal. Unification does, however, succeed using the second clause for `q/2` giving a substitution `{Y/2}`. The current goal is now empty and the resolution procedure succeeds and terminates.

An "interpretation" of a logic program consists of some domain of discourse over which variables can range. All constants of the program are assigned an element of the domain. All functions are assigned a mapping over the domain. All predicates are assigned a relation on the domain. All quantifiers and connectives have an *apriori* fixed meaning. Thus an interpretation is used to give meaning for every symbol in a program. An interpretation in which a formula expresses a true statement is said to be a "model" of the formula. The programmer usually has an interpretation in mind when writing a program. This is the "intended interpretation", which, if it meets the specification, will be a model.

Consider the formula $\forall X\ \exists Y\ p(X, Y)$ and the interpretation *I* where the domain of discourse is the non-negative integers and `p` is assigned the relation $<$. *I* is then a model for the formula, as the formula expresses the true statement that "for every non-negative integer, there exists another non-negative integer which is strictly greater than the chosen integer".

The declarative semantics of a logic program is given by characterising a particular model of the program. Intuitively, this is the one containing the minimal amount of information whilst still remaining a model. This is because any extra information in the model can only reflect on formulas which are not derivable from the program and thus, are irrelevant. This model is known as the "least model".

A set of clauses `S` is said to be "satisfiable" if there is an interpretation which is a model for `S`. Assume a logic program `P` and a goal clause `G`, then the problem is determining the unsatisfiability of `P ∪ {G}`. This would seem to imply that every interpretation of `P ∪ {G}` must not be a model. There are, however, an infinite number of possible interpretations and it would not be feasible to verify that all of them give rise to unsatisfiability.

Fortunately, it is possible to identify a smaller class of interpretations which need only be considered. These are known as "Herbrand interpretations" [77]. Informally a Herbrand interpretation is one in which the domain of discourse consists of all the symbols present in the program. Each symbol maps to itself, and variables range over the symbols, and terms which can be constructed from these symbols.

Consider the program below

```
p(X) ← q(f(a),g(X)).
r(Y) ←.
```

We now give its Herbrand Interpretation. The domain of discourse is the set

```
{a, f(a), g(a), f(f(a)), f(g(a)), g(f(a)), g(g(a)), ...}
```

Constants are assigned themselves; thus `a` is assigned `a`. The functions `f` and `g` are assigned themselves taking arguments from the domain of discourse.

This property effectively means that deduction systems only have to work at the level of symbol manipulation and do not have to worry about what the user might have intended the symbols constituting the program to mean.

A Herbrand Interpretation for a program which is a model is a "Herbrand Model". The meaning of a logic program should consist of just those formulas which are logically implied by the program. The declarative semantics of a program are therefore given by the "least Herbrand model". This consists of just those atoms which are logical consequences of the program.

This underlying mathematics provides a formal basis for the construction of correct programs. This in turn implies there are sound methods for proving properties of programs and enables transformation methods to be developed. A typical application is the transformation of a program, written merely as a prototype specification of a solution to a problem, into a more efficient semantically equivalent one.

The standard unification procedures utilised by most Prolog implementations are purely syntactic. Terms are equal if they are syntactically identical with the appropriate unifying substitution applied. However, because of logic programming's mathematical foundations, it is possible to develop new types of languages called "constraint logic programming languages" [173] [82] [50] [51], which enable the user to supply a constraint-solver which works in the user's intended domain of interpretation, for example real numbers. This, together with the current work on implementation, will lead to the development of more powerful logic programming systems than those around today.

Developments in Prolog Implementation

The development of logic programming owes much to the programming language Prolog [34]. In 1972 Phillipe Roussel designed the first Prolog interpreter at the Université d'Aix Marseilles. In fact, the name Prolog was suggested by Roussel's wife Jacqueline, as an abbreviation for *programmation en logique*. It was written in Algol-W and employed the clause-copying technique. This means that whenever a clause is selected as a candidate for reduction, a copy of it is made. This is a simple, albeit inefficient, method of avoiding name clashes with variables. Roussel then visited Edinburgh and learned of Boyer and Moore's structure-sharing approach for representing data structures [11]. Using this method, data structures are represented as skeletons with an associated set of variables which can be instantiated later. This way the skeleton of a data structure can be shared leaving the creation and binding of variables as the only expense. On returning to Marseilles, Roussel started work together with two of his students, H. Meloni and G. Battani, on a Fortran version of the original interpreter using structure sharing [132].

The next major implementation breakthrough was made by David H.D. Warren at the University of Edinburgh. He developed a native code compiler for Prolog [174]. The target architecture was a DEC-10. The implementation was based around a multi-stack abstract machine and used the structure-sharing technique. He later developed the idea of tail recursion optimisation, whereby the space used by a calling goal can be reused if the clause is determinate by the time the last body goal is called.

On moving to the Stanford Research Institute, in California, Warren worked on the development of an improved abstract machine for the efficient execution of Prolog. This was called "The Old Engine". The system comprises a compiler to a Prolog abstract instruction set and a corresponding abstract machine emulator. It employed full structure-copying and goal stacking, whereby all goals making up the current resolvant lie on a stack. The topmost element of this stack represents the next body goal to be solved when the current body goal succeeds. An advantage of this method is that there is no need to create an environment to hold variable bindings for a clause. Full structure-copying means that every time a new data structure is created, any data that is sharable is not shared, but is in fact copied. These two design decisions make the implementation much simpler than the older DEC-10 design.

What was originally called "The New Engine" and "Warren Abstract Machine" (WAM) was developed next [175]. This also employed structure copying, but only for data structures and not goals. The goals can be thought of as being represented in a structure sharing manner. As well as holding choice points on the local stack, this model also has to manage environments; that is, information which needs to be remembered across procedure calls. The WAM now forms the basis of many commercial Prolog implementations. This work was further expanded by Evan Tick who examined the influences of the abstract instruction set on possible microarchitectures [164].

There are advantages and disadvantages of both the "Old" and "New" models. There are no environments associated with the "Old" model, hence the implementation and garbage collection process is much simpler. Tail recursion optimisation is much easier to achieve in the "Old" model. A calling goal can simply be discarded if it is younger than the most recent choice point. All the variables in a clause can be held in machine registers in the "Old" model. The code for a clause will no longer be referenced once resolution with it has completed. In the "New" model this is not the case and the code area tends to be accessed randomly, creating inefficiencies when interacting with a virtual memory system. In general, the compiled code for a clause in the "New" model will contain jumps. This will tend to reduce performance on pipelined hardware.

In the "Old" goal stacking model however, whenever a clause is selected as a candidate for reduction it is copied. If the clause should fail early then a lot of copying has been done unnecessarily. This is avoided in the environment stacking "New" model. In the "New" model the top of the stack is normally buffered in machine registers to increase performance. In the "Old" model the stack size is much less stable rendering this optimisation less profitable. In the "Old" model when popping off goals there may be a problem with dangling references pointing to this now discarded area. This implies the need for a check to be applied on the whereabouts of an object every time a variable is bound to that object. The goal stacking representation is less compact than the environment stacking representation implying a less efficient model in memory performance criteria.

Since the Japanese declared their Fifth Generation Computing Programme there has been much widespread activity in the development of faster implementations and actual hardware to support Prolog. There is an active research group at the University of California at Berkeley who developed the PLM [53] [149], an extended version of Warren's New Model. This has subsequently been turned into a commercial product and is being marketed by Xenologic Inc. The architecture is called the X-1 [129] [53] [48], and currently consists of two VME boards which plug into the backplane of a Sun Microsystems workstation. Other work in the U.S.A. includes the development of a VLSI RISC Architecture for the execution of Prolog being developed by the LOW RISC group at Arizona State University [101] [146].

Japanese Prolog hardware developments include the Co-Operative High Performance Sequential Inference Machine (CHI-II) [74] [93] produced by NEC; the Integrated Prolog Processor (IPP) [1] [2] [183] produced by Hitachi; joint research by ICOT and Mitsubishi Electric Corp. developing the Personal Sequential Inference Machine (PSI-I [102] [109] [154] [156] [168] [186] and PSI-II [103]); PEGASUS [139], a Prolog Oriented RISC Processor designed by Mitsubishi Electric Corp.; and The High-Speed Prolog Machine (HPM) [104], developed jointly by NEC Corp. and ICOT. There is also a project at the National Chiao-Tung University in China developing a RISC-type Prolog

Machine (RPM) [24].

Research in Europe includes the development of a series of architectures by ECRC culminating in the Inference Crunching Machine (ICM4) which is now being developed further into the Knowledge Crunching Machine (KCM) [110] [152]. There is also work at British Aerospace, England, developing the Declarative Language Machine (DLM) [12] [120]. There is a group at the Politecnico di Torino, Italy, working on a VLSI implementation of a Prolog Interpreter [26] [27].

Computer Architecture Developments

There has been a great deal of research into attempting to improve the execution speed of computers through the exploitation of parallelism. Commercially produced parallel computer architectures are now available and are becoming commonplace in universities and industry. The most successful of these include the Sequent Balance [140], BBN Butterfly [165], [10], and Intel Hypercube [81].

Despite the parallel hardware the actual model of computation as far as the user is concerned is still very heavily weighted to the classic von-Neumann computer. If the imperative programmer wishes to write explicit parallel programs, he/she now has to worry about parallelising these sequences into different execution streams in addition to all the usual burdens of sequencing commands. Synchronization becomes a big issue because of the frequent use of destructive assignment in imperative programs. He, or she, now has to ensure that any communication between different portions of a program, designated as concurrent, do not outweigh any gains that, in theory, have come from the parallelism. This undesirable effect may be resolved by the use of declarative programming languages to prevent the programmer from making an incorrect choice of load balancing algorithm for the parallel execution of his/her program.

Parallelism in Logic Programs

As a prelude to the next section, the exploitation and pitfalls of the two major forms of parallelism present in logic programs will now be discussed. These are "Or-Parallelism" and "And-Parallelism".

A resolution step consists of selecting a literal from the current goal and unifying it with the heads all of the clauses for its defining procedure. In a conventional Prolog implementation, the clauses would be searched, and solved, in the sequence that they are written down. In theory there is no reason why all of the clauses should not be solved at the same time. This form of parallelism is called "Or-Parallelism".

As an example consider the following goal clause and set of program clauses

```
← p(X, Y).

p(1, Y) ← q1(Y).
p(2, Y) ← q2(Y).
p(3, Y) ← q3(Y).
```

It is possible, if machine resources and the implementation allow, to spawn off a separate process to solve the query with respect to each of the program clauses. Each clause is able to bind the variables in the calling goal to different terms. In this case the variable `X` will be bound to `1`, `2`, and `3`. The variable `Y` likewise may be bound to distinct terms by the procedures `q1`, `q2`, and `q3`.

If Or-Parallelism is to be exploited then it is necessary to support some form of multiple environment management scheme to keep any different solution spaces separate from each other. For this form of parallelism to be profitable, there should be a reasonable amount of work associated with at least two of the clauses to combat the overhead of spawning the separate processes for each piece of work and the possible creation and management of their individual binding environments.

Another possibility for parallelism is to solve several atoms of the current resolvant simultaneously. This is known as exploiting "And-Parallelism" and can result in having several sets of several processes, with each set working on the same solution if it is combined with Or-Parallelism.

The following goal clause and set of program clauses illustrates this form of parallelism and the associated implementation difficulties.

```
← p(X, Y), q(Y, Z).

p(1, 1).
p(1, 2).
p(2, 1).
p(2, 2).
```

```
q(2, 1).
q(2, 2).
q(3, 1).
q(3, 2).
```

There are two solutions, `{X/1, Y/2, Z/1}` and `{X/2, Y/2, Z/2}`. The variable `Y` is shared by more than one literal. It is possible for each literal to bind a shared variable to conflicting terms, implying the need for a mechanism to resolve conflicting bindings.

Concurrent Logic Programming

As the state-of-the-art hardware technology reaches its fundamental limits, it will become necessary to take advantage of parallelism if faster performance is to be achieved by providing implementations of programming languages that run in parallel on parallel computer architectures. In critical real-time applications, and in problems which are naturally expressed in a concurrent manner, the programmer will want to communicate to the computer any opportunities for exploiting parallelism but only when it is known to be desirable. It should be possible to accomplish this without burdening the programmer. A possible solution for both of these goals may be the use of a programming formalism which has a declarative reading yet which allows the programmer to use annotation to guide the computer to recognise this parallelism.

The family of concurrent logic programming languages appear to be the most appropriate candidates for this job since they enable programs to retain a declarative reading and allow the programmer to express parallelism. Proposed dialects include Guarded Horn Clauses, commonly referred to as GHC [170] [157], Concurrent Prolog [142] [143], P-Prolog [184] [185], CP [134] [136], and Parlog [73].

Logic programs are non-deterministic by nature. There are two forms of non-determinism, of which at least one is exploited by the logic programming languages mentioned above. Where there are multiple solutions to a query, but the logic programming system does not know which is needed, it exploits "don't-know non-determinism". It can either backtrack through all of the solutions in turn, exploit Or-Parallelism, or use some combination of both techniques.

The other form of non-determinism, and the one most prevalent in concurrent logic programming, is "don't-care non-determinism". A single solution is required and the system does not care which one it is. This places a burden upon the programmer to ensure that if a computation path is selected, which could possibly have given a correct answer but which actually led to failure, then no other computation path would have led to a success.

One common property among all these concurrent logic programming languages is that of enforcing upon the user the rigid programming style mentioned above. Moreover, this is a style where the programmer has to be aware of the notion of "committed-choice non-determinism". The non-determinism part comes from the fact that the calling goal can unify with the head of more than one clause. The committed-choice part implies that out of the set of these "candidate clauses" only one is chosen for further reduction.

All programs written in this subset of logic programming languages consist of "guarded clauses". The body of each clause is split into two parts; the "guard" and the "body". These are both conjunctions of literals. They are separated by a "commit" symbol. A guarded clause takes the syntactic form, `H ← G : B`, where `H` is the head literal, `G` is the guard conjunction, `B` is the body conjunction, and `:` is the commit operator. The operational semantics of guarded clauses varies from language to language. If none of the guard goals is a call to a user-defined relation then the clause is said to be "flat", otherwise it is a "non-flat" clause. All of the languages previously mentioned are "non-flat", that is, they allow the user to be able to specify "non-flat" clauses.

In the following description of the different operational semantics of these languages, it is necessary to make the distinction between variables of the "call" and variables in the selected clause. The "call" is the selected goal in the goal clause being used as a candidate for resolution with the selected clause. If the unification of the call with the head of the selected clause is successful, and all the guard goals also succeed, then the clause is a "candidate", and can then be selected for further computation, i.e. the reduction of the body goals.

Guarded Horn Clauses

Guarded Horn Clauses (GHC) is the most syntactically clean of all the programming languages mentioned; no additional syntax is needed. Computation proceeds by attempting to reduce all the goals in the goal clause, conceptually in parallel, though the way this is achieved is implementation-dependent and it is up to the implementation to provide this illusion of parallelism, that is of all goals in a goal clause concurrently executing. A call will attempt to unify successfully with all possible clause heads. If any of these attempted unifications fail, then the clause in question is discarded from the set of potential candidate clauses. If the unification would succeed if any of the variables in the call were bound, then the unification suspends waiting for the call variable to be instantiated whereupon it is reawoken and the unification process reactivated. If the unification succeeds then the clause becomes a candidate. If none of the unifications succeed but there are suspended unifications then the call suspends. If none of the unification processes succeed or suspend but instead all of them fail, then the call will fail. If there are any candidate clauses available then one is chosen nondeterministically for further reduction. The body goals take the place of the original call goal in the goal clause.

Concurrent Prolog

Syntactically Concurrent Prolog consists of guarded clauses with an additional annotation used to mark variables as being "read-only". A goal containing a read-only variable as an argument, or contained in a subterm of one of its arguments, cannot proceed until that variable has been instantiated. Unification processes suspend on read-only variables; the unification process is not (abstractly) affected by the particular environment location of variables. Unification conceptually proceeds by taking a copy of the call environment for every clause of the relation in question. Unification then proceeds as normal, but with each process using its own copy of the call environment in which to do output binding. If both the unification process and the guard computation are successful then "back unification" takes place. The copied environment, now probably modified, is unified against the original calling environment; this unification process must be atomic. If this unification is successful then the clause becomes a candidate; otherwise the unification and guard computation fails. This "back unification" is required because every unification process takes a copy of its calling environment, and the original call environment may have been updated by other goals in the goal clause. A candidate is then non-deterministically chosen and reduction of the body goals proceeds.

P-Prolog

P-Prolog also exploits don't-care non-determinism but, unlike all the other languages covered here, also allows the user the facility of don't-know non-determinism. P-Prolog uses "exclusive clauses" as a committed-choice mechanism.

Consider the relation defined by the following set of clauses,

```
H1 ← G1 : B1. (C1)
 .     .
 .     .
Hn ← Gn : Bn. (Cn)
```

Let the relation `unifiable(H, P)` denote the fact that `H` can be unified with a goal `P`. For a goal `P`, the clauses `C1`, ..., `Cn` are "exclusive" if and only if the following holds :

```
EXC(unifiable(H1, P) ∧ {G1}S1, ..., unifiable(Hn, P) ∧ {Gn}Sn)
```

where `Si` is the unifier for `P` with `Hi` and `EXC` is defined by :

```
EXC(F1, F2) ← (F1 ∧ ~ F2) ∨ (~ F1 ∧ F2)
```

That is, if one of the related formulas is true, all of the others are false.

A set of guarded clauses is exclusive for `P` if and only if there is only one committable clause for `P`. A logic programming system trying to reduce a goal `P` will first check that any sets of exclusive clauses only have one clause that is committable. If this is not the case then the goal will suspend for these clauses, pending instantiation of argument variables.

P-Prolog also allows the user to make use of don't-know non-determinism through "non-exclusive clauses". This allows a logic programming system to exploit any Or-Parallelism thus provided. A set of clauses is "non-exclusive" for a goal if and only if at least one pair of clauses in this set are not exclusive. In P-Prolog all non-exclusive clauses will potentially be executed in parallel with any committed exclusive clause.

It is up to the programmer to tell the system which are the "expected exclusive clauses" for a relation. All of the clauses for a procedure are divided into subsets. Each of the clauses in different subsets are expected, by the system, to be exclusive. Clauses in the same subset are not expected to be exclusive. The subsets are indicated syntactically by using different implication operators. A subset in which there is only one clause is indicated by `:-` and is called a "single neck clause". A subset consisting of more than one clause is indicated by `:--`, `:---`, ... etc. These are known as "double neck clauses", "triple neck clauses" etc. An exclusive check occurs between all "single neck clauses" and all clauses with different implication operators.

There are three different kinds of action that can be taken when trying to reduce a goal in a P-Prolog system. The goal can fail if all of its alternative clauses are not committable. It will suspend if there is more than one committable expected exclusive clause. It will succeed when all of the expected exclusive clauses satisfy the exclusive relation.

CP

CP is in fact, a family of concurrent logic programming languages. The variety is denoted by the selection of various control operators. These specialised simple operators are discussed individually below.

It is possible for goals to share variables. Because of this these goals can instantiate variables to conflicting terms. A successful implementation of CP which handled this problem would be required to gather all solutions from each sharing goal and then join them up consistently. In a programming language in which it is required to be able to express operating system constructs, the overheads would be too expensive. A "wait" annotation, ↓ is introduced to solve this problem. This effectively restricts one goal to be the producer of a top-level binding for a variable and all the other goals sharing the variable to be consumers. The annotation can be applied to any term appearing in the head of a clause. A goal can ↓-unify successfully with the head of a clause if and only if all ↓-decorated terms in the head unify against non-variables in the goal. If ↓-unification succeeds then the normal unification mechanism proceeds. ↓-unification will suspend if there is a variable term in the goal and its corresponding argument in the head of the clause is a ↓-decorated term. ↓-unification will eventually fail if the use the normal unification algorithm can proceed but leads to failure.

CP also provides the programmer with a set of three commit operators; the "don't care" commit, `|`, and two "don't know" operators, one parallel, `&`, and one sequential, `&&`. These operators differ only in their actions taken against any of their active Or-siblings. The "don't care" operator, | kills all of its Or-siblings. This operator has the same semantics as the commit operators in all of the other programming languages mentioned.

In the parallel "don't know" case the Or-siblings are allowed to carry on computing. However, they carry on executing with respect to a different copy of the system configuration as it is at this point in time. The effect of this is very much as if two CP machines are forked at the point of commitment; one is executing the body goals of the committed clause along with the other original goal atoms, and the other machine is executing with the other Or-sibling clause processes and the other original goal literals.

The sequential "don't know" operator "freezes" all of its Or-siblings. If the clause chosen should eventually lead to failure then the CP system will backtrack to a point where a sequential "don't know" commit operator was executed and reawaken the frozen computations.

CP also allows the programmer to specify when clauses should be tried in sequence and not in parallel. The "sequential-Or" and "sequential-And" operators are both denoted by ;. If two clauses are separated by a "sequential-Or" operator then the second clause can only be tried if the first one commits. If the commit operator was then the second clause will never be tried as the commitment effectively kills it before an attempted reduction can be started. If the commit operator was & then the second clause will be tried immediately. If the commit operator was && then the second clause can be tried on backtracking.

Literals in a goal clause, and in the guard or body of a program clause, can be designated as having to be executed sequentially. This is exactly the same behaviour exhibited in a conventional Prolog implementation. To indicate this the programmer makes use of a "sequential-And" operator denoted by ;. The goals after the "sequential-And" operator will only be reduced after successful reduction of all of the goals preceding ;.

Parlog

Parlog is another member of the committed-choice logic programming language family. A detailed description of its syntactical form and operational semantics is given in chapter 2. Its operational characteristics are highlighted here for completeness.

It has only one "don't care" commitment operator, :. On commitment of a clause process, all of its active Or-siblings are killed. It is up to the programmer to ensure that there is no possibility of achieving conflicting bindings of shared variables. Process synchronisation is achieved through the use of "mode declarations". There is one mode declaration for every Parlog procedure, in which there is one symbol per argument. An argument can be designated as an "input", ?, or as an "output", ↑. If an argument is an input and the corresponding goal argument would unify with it if some of its variables were instantiated, then the unification would suspend. If an argument is designated as an output then any bindings made for it can only occur in execution of the body literals of the clause.

Implementation Difficulties

There are implementation difficulties associated with all of the above mentioned concurrent logic programming languages. A GHC implementation must be able to distinguish the context of variables, whether they belong to a goal or are local to a clause. This is so that the system can tell whether a unification should suspend or not. This is a run-time property and cannot be determined at compile-time. Every time a guard process attempts to bind a variable, a check must be made to see if it is in the call environment or the clause's local environment. In the implementation, this would mean that environments would have to be "coloured" in order for processes to distinguish between them. In the implementation this means that variables are tagged with a so-called "read-only" level that can be arbitrarily large. If a variable-instance is a structure sent from guard to body (commitment) then all coloured variables in this structure must have their associated levels decremented. This operation implies traversing the whole structure. Recent results seem to indicate that this "colouring" of environments can be quite expensive [94] [89].

Concurrent Prolog involves the creation of multiple environments when attempting unification of goals with clause heads [98]. This is because guards are systems of And-Parallel goals which can, in turn, unify with heads of clauses which can then, in turn, execute guards and so on. This leads on to the situation of having to manage hierarchical goal systems and binding environments. The burden of all this has to be carried by the commitment mechanism. All bindings to non read-only variables, made in a goal's environment after the spawning of a unification, will not be visible to that goal until commitment since the call environment will have been copied.

There are many inconsistencies associated with the operational semantics of Concurrent Prolog [135] [169]. The semantics of the interaction of read-only variables with copied binding environments is not specified in [142]. A variable which is non-read-only at the time of spawning will be copied into the unification process's environment. Before commitment, however, the original call variable may be bound to a read-only variable. The question of whether any further instantiations are seen by the copy of the variable is not specified. The operational semantics of Concurrent Prolog state that if a non-read-only variable is bound to a read-only variable then the result is a read-only variable; this would appear to be the case here. This would mean that a lot of redundant effort could be expended on unifying goals with heads of clauses, and their subsequent guard computations, if they do not eventually lead to a solution, because of a failure during the back-commit phase. If the information had been transmitted immediately, the unnecessary work would not have happened.

V.J. Saraswat proposes "eager commitment" as a possible solution to this problem. Commitment has to be atomic according to its semantics. On commitment any bindings made by the committing goal to the call environment are broadcast to any other sibling guard systems. The view taken in the research described by this thesis, is that this would be too expensive in a highly-parallel system and would detract from Concurrent Prolog's claim to be an effective formalism for describing efficient concurrent communicating systems of processes. One consequence of this back-propagation of bindings at committment, is that active goals can be frozen unexpectedly by other sibling goals binding shared variables to read-only variables, thus potentially suspending sibling guard computations. The read-only annotation is an operational feature and programs containing such annotations are not subject to a static semantic analysis of their correctness. This seems highly undesirable and, for this reason, Concurrent Prolog is not considered further.

P-Prolog allows both And- and Or-Parallelism; the management of both these forms of parallelism seems expensive. According to [184] an interpreter for P-Prolog has been written in C-Prolog to evaluate the programming language. It is conjectured that "single neck" and "double neck" clauses are sufficient for all practical purposes and thus the implementation supports only this set of annotations. The development of a C interpreter for P-Prolog is reviewed in [185] but no concrete results are given, and a compiler for P-

Prolog is mentioned as future work.

The author of this book is not aware of any real implementation of CP. In V.J. Saraswat's thesis proposal, [134], it is mentioned that a uniprocessor implementation would be developed along the lines of SPM, Logix and the PPM implementation (described later in chapter 5). A short-term implementation was discussed whereby K. Ueda's Concurrent Prolog to Prolog compiler would be modified but no details are reported. A real parallel implementation would suffer from the same problems as that of Concurrent Prolog. Multiple copies of binding environments have to be managed, one per possible matching clause; and on commitment the unification of the copied environment with the original call environment has to be atomic. This would create severe burdens on a parallel implementation supposedly supporting an efficient concurrent programming language. In addition CP places great emphasis on the user annotating programs in order to ensure their correctness, which seems unreasonable.

Flat Concurrent Logic Programming Languages

As a result of the above mentioned implementation difficulties there have been several restricted versions of some of these programming languages proposed. These include Flat Concurrent Prolog, commonly referred to as FCP [100] [147], Safe Concurrent Prolog [35], Oc [153], FLENG Prolog [107] [108], and Flat GHC [91] [90]. These are briefly reviewed below.

FCP is a restricted subset of Concurrent Prolog where the use of guard predicates is confined to the use of pre-defined test predicates. This alleviates the need for supporting hierarchical multiple environments. Safe Concurrent Prolog, SCP, imposes an added restriction to Concurrent Prolog in that variables which can be bound in the calling environment are annotated.

This new annotation is called "write-enable" and is represented syntactically by ↑. It is used to distinguish "input" from "output" variables in the head of a clause, in a similar way to Parlog mode declarations, but refers to variables and not arguments and is thus more flexible. Output variables are those annotated with ↑, any others are designated as "input" by default. This statically determines which variables a guard system can instantiate. It states which call environment variables are accessible to the guard and which are not, the safety restriction being that guards are not allowed to write upon input variables.

Unfortunately, the problem of whether a program conforms to its syntactic specification is undecidable. An SCP implementation would still have to manage multiple hierarchical environments but it is now known which variables can be instantiated so the mechanism should be simpler and more efficient. By means of partially evaluating an SCP interpreter, written in FCP, with respect to an SCP program it is possible to transform any correct SCP program into an equivalent FCP program. Thus we can extend the syntactic class of the Concurrent Prolog family of languages implementable, without having to manage multiple hierarchical environments.

FGHC is based on the same design principles as FCP. Once again the user is restricted to a set of pre-defined test guard predicates to avoid the creation of multiple hierarchical binding environments. It has been adopted as the kernel parallel programming language, known as KL1, for the Japanese fifth generation computing effort. An abstract machine has been developed and is reported in [88]. The KL1 is compiled down into an idealised KL1 instruction set called KL1-B and can then be executed on a variety of parallel machines such as the Multi-PSI [91] [155] and PIM [138]. Oc can be thought of as FGHC without guards, thus affording very efficient implementation, but the class of programs which can be expressed in the programming language is very restrictive and hence Oc is not mentioned further.

FLENG Prolog is also a committed-choice programming language but is devoid of guards. Commitment is able to take place as soon as a head unification operation has successfully completed. The suspension mechanism is exactly the same as in GHC. Unlike any of the other concurrent logic programming languages discussed, the `unify/3` procedure makes explicit the result of its operation. A `compute/4` relation is used to evaluate operations which are supposed to resemble that of the underlying machine. It seems possible to translate a larger subset of GHC than that of FGHC into FLENG Prolog. In order for the language to be efficient, it appears necessary to implement it on a vector architecture and so it is not a candidate for efficient portable concurrent programming. Thus it is not considered any more.

It is extremely hard to express solutions to AI-type problems with a flat language [181] such as FCP, FGHC, Oc and FLENG Prolog. It is for this reason that in future chapters we are considering only Parlog. It is non-flat and any annotation is restricted to mode declarations. This makes it possible to determine the possible behaviour of a Parlog program at compile-time and also allows us to reason about it with confidence. It is not an inherently safe language in that it is possible to write clauses in which the evaluation of the guard causes variables in the calling goal to become instantiated. It is possible to detect most potentially unsafe clauses. Its implementation does not pose any of the difficulties mentioned above. It does not require a mechanism to support multiple hierarchical environments and distinguish the whereabouts in these environments of variables at run time. Hence it is the most likely to execute efficiently, and still provide the user with a formalism for expressing concurrent solutions to problems.

Objectives and Contributions of this Research

Concurrent logic programming languages have been proposed as method of programming concurrent algorithms in a declarative manner. The objective of this research is to devise, compare, and contrast possible efficient parallel implementation models for concurrent logic programming languages. In particular, it was decided to concentrate on the programming language Parlog, as it is the most likely of the family of non-flat concurrent logic programming languages to produce an efficient implementation because it does not require a variable-location check to be made at run-time.

Two different architectural models, a Packet-Rewriting model and a Multi-Sequential model are considered and software simulators built for each (both written in C). The Packet-Rewriting model was conceived as result of the work on packet-rewriting models for functional languages [72], [179]. Functional languages are very similar to concurrent logic programming languages and it was hoped that the same computational model would support both programming paradigms efficiently. New forms of packet are added to support the logic programming paradigm. The original model did not support logical variables and did not provide the functionality to provide separate copies of packets needed to support different binding environments for each guard of a predicate. The returning of values to suspended packets mechanism is extended to provide a method for guards to commit.

Under simulation, however, it was found that the Packet-Rewriting model did not perform well. Two benchmarks were run, one which tested the raw performance of a processor and another which was very highly parallel. The model produced very good performance figures for the very highly parallel benchmark but used a large number of processors to achieve the results. The performance of each single processor was poor and not cost-effective except perhaps for those programmers that are purely interested in how fast their applications run independent of the cost. The peak performance of the processors was limited due to the large number of reads and writes to memory associated with each rewrite. It seems only possible to achieve a speed of two orders of magnitude less than that of a conventional Prolog implementation.

As a result of the simulation of the Packet-Rewriting model, the Multi-Sequential model was designed because of the inefficiencies encountered in the Packet-Rewriting model. This computational model seeks to exploit current WAM technology by basing itself upon an architecture constructed of multiple WAM-like engines, tailored for Parlog execution. The unit of work in the Multi-Sequential model is of a much more coarser-grain than that of the Packet-Rewriting model. In the Packet-Rewriting model case, the units of work have no relation to each other; each one is considered as equal a candidate to be executed as any other. In The Multi-Sequential model the work unit is part of a branch of a computation tree. This model proved to be more cost-effective than the finer-grained Packet-Rewriting model in that the raw performance of a processor was much larger.

Then various issues concerning the implementation of a parallel logic language, with emphasis on Parlog, on these models are examined at length. Finally, possible improvements and outstanding issues which need to be resolved in the paradigm of concurrent logic programming are discussed.

Preview of Book Contents

Chapter 2 contains a description of the concurrent logic programming language Parlog. The usefulness of Parlog as a declarative medium for specifying concurrent systems is stressed by means of several small representative example programs. There is also a comparison with other proposals such as GHC and Concurrent Prolog where it is appropriate. We also outline the compilation of Parlog to a more architectural-sympathetic medium called KP-And-Or-Tree. It is this intermediate language which will be implemented.

Chapter 3 presents an overview of the Packet-Rewriting computational model which is independent of Parlog. The model is based on the idea of computation as graph rewriting where each node of the graph is represented as a packet. The basic model is biased towards the implementation of functional programming languages but is sufficiently flexible to allow the implementation of logic programming styles and even imperative ideas.

Chapter 4 builds upon the Packet-Rewriting model presented in the previous chapter. We discuss the features that need to be present in a fine-grain implementation of Parlog and their integration into the Packet-Rewriting model. We also compare the approach with that of the ALICE implementation at Imperial College [95], which was developed at the same time as the model described in this chapter.

Chapter 5 presents an alternative form of computational model. The approach is a more concrete form of model based on a coarse-grain multiple execution-agent approach. The resulting implementation is known as the PPM, the *Parallel Parlog Machine*. The PPM builds upon the implementation of the SPM, the *Sequential Parlog Machine*, designed at Imperial College using it as the sequential part of the PPM. The agents consist of local memory and an execution unit. However, the collection of local memory modules in the system is considered as being globally addressable.

Chapter 6 summarises and discusses the work and draws conclusions of use to other implementors. Unresolved issues are also discussed and possible further work is outlined.

Chapter 2 Parlog A Concurrent Logic Programming Language

Introduction

The programming language Parlog is representative of the current trend towards the efficient use of parallel computer architectures. Like most other logic programming languages, it has semantic foundations based upon first order predicate logic. It is a programming language which allows the user to express concepts of concurrency while still endeavouring to remain within a declarative framework. Specifically the concepts considered fundamental are: concurrency, communication, indeterminacy and synchronization. Parlog's operational semantics are essentially a form of resolution-based theorem proving.

The aim is to provide the user with an efficient first-order-logic based programming language. This is achieved by only exploiting stream And-Parallelism and a limited form of Or-Parallelism, through the use of "mode declarations" and "don't-care non-determinism", which are explained below. Parlog avoids the problems associated with the binding of shared variables by dependent And-processes, and with the management of multiple, conceptually independent, environments needed to handle Or-Parallelism which is inherent in other non-flat concurrent logic programming languages.

Concurrency

The concept of concurrency is embodied in Parlog by the so-called process interpretation of logic. A goal clause consists of a number of literals. In this interpretation each literal is thought of as an individual process. A goal clause then represents a system of concurrent processes. This is also how And-Parallelism is exploited in a Parlog implementation.

Inter-Process Communication

Goal clause literals which share variables are dependent upon each other. In the process interpretation, dependent goal clause literals can be thought of as being in a process group. The processes making up a process group are called dependent processes. The shared variables of a process group are interpreted as communication channels. For example, consider the goal clause resolvant shown below

```
← p(X, Y) // q(Y, Z) // r(Z, X).
```

The arrow symbol, ←, is the syntax for logical implication. All variables are denoted by symbols beginning with a capital letter, all other symbols are constants. There are three literals `p/2`, `q/2`, and `r/2` making up the resolvant, hence a system of three process. The `//` symbol is the syntax used to denote a "parallel-And" conjunction. The literals separated by a parallel-And are to be executed in parallel, or pseudo-parallel if the program is running on a sequential implementation of Parlog. There are three shared variables, `X`, `Y`, and `Z`, hence three communication channels. For instance, the processes `p/2` and `q/2` share the variable `Y` which they will use to communicate with each other.

Processes communicate using a technique known as "incomplete messages" or "back communication". This is possible because of the "logical variable" property present in logic programming languages. A process that wishes to communicate information to another process will bind the shared variable to a nonground nonvariable term. The variables of this term can then be subsequently used by the receiving process to reply. Consider the following example "conversation" between the processes `p/2` and `q/2` in the above system.

1. `p/2` binds `Y` to the term `[hello|Y1]`
2. `q/2` sees the hello message and replies by binding the variable `Y1` to the term `[hello|Y2]`
3. `p/2` sees the acknowledgement from `q/2` and then sends some information by binding `Y2` to the term `[info|Y3]`
4. `q/2` then acknowledges receipt of the information by binding `Y3` to `[ack|Y4]`
5. `p/2` then sees `q/2` has received the information and closes the conversation by binding `Y4` to `[]`

As can be seen from the above example the usual form of communication is conducted by binding successive variables to incomplete lists. To close a communication channel it is only necessary to bind the appropriate shared variable to a ground term. It is usual to use the nil list, `[]`, since lists are used to represent the communication stream.

Indeterminacy

Computer systems in the real world have to be able to deal with indeterminacy. There are two forms of non-determinism, "don't-know" and "don't-care". In the case of don't-know non-determinism, it is the case that before attempting to find the set of possible solutions for a process the number of possible solutions is unknown. To implement don't-know non-determinism requires an implementation of Or-Parallelism in order that a choice can be made. It is possible that executing some clauses can suspend the computation while there may be clauses existing that can produce a satisfactory solution. The non-determinism can be obtained by employing pseudo-Or-Parallelism, using a backtracking mechanism, or a full parallel implementation, or possibly a combination of both. In order to enable an efficient implementation of a logic programming language to be developed, Parlog sacrifices full Or-Parallelism.

Parlog seeks only to exploit don't-care non-determinism. In this case only one of a set of solutions is selected non-deterministically and the programmer does not care which one. The concept of guards [80] is introduced to model this feature. Every clause in a Parlog program is guarded as shown in the example relation below.

```
H1  ←  G1  :  B1 \\
H2  ←  G2  :  B2 \\
H3  ←  G3  :  B3.
```

There are three clauses making up the `H` relation. The antecedent of each clause consists of two parts, the guard and the body. The guards and bodies in the above relation are `G1`, `G2`, `G3`, and `B1`, `B2`, `B3` respectively. The guard is separated from the body by the guard conjunction symbol `:`. Declaratively this can be read as a logical conjunction symbol. The `\\` symbol implies that the sets of clauses it separates should be used by the calling goal process to spawn off corresponding sets of parallel clause processes. The guard and body of a clause consist of conjunctions of literals, as in the case of conventional Horn clause logic. A goal clause conjunct will attempt to reduce itself by first unifying with the heads of each clause in its defining relation. For each successful head unification, the process then attempts to reduce its guard system. For each of these clauses whose guard system is satisfied the clause becomes a "candidate". A clause is then chosen non-deterministically from this candidate set. The body goals of this clause then replace the original goal process in the goal system of processes. It is this feature which gives the programmer a restricted form of Or-Parallelism (parallel execution of guards).

Synchronization

In order to make processes wait for a response from another process, the programming language must enable the user to specify that a process should not attempt to bind a variable to a nonvariable term but should await its instantiation. This mechanism can also be used to ensure that all shared variables are only bound by one process. This in turn will lead to an efficient implementation of And-Parallelism, as there will be no need to join sets of bindings of shared variables together to produce consistent solutions to a conjunction.

In the normal unification algorithm [130], a most general unifier is sought for a set of terms. In the reduction process, the number of terms is two, one argument in the calling goal in the goal clause and the corresponding argument of a clause in the defining relation. The calling goal is allowed to bind variables in the defining clause; bindings are allowed for variables in goal clause by matching against terms in the defining clause. Thus unification can be thought of as a form of two-way pattern matching. As an example consider the two terms `p(X, 3, Y)` and `p(4, Z, Z)`. The most general unifier is `{ X/4, Z/3, Y/Z }`. The variable in the first term, `X`, has been bound to the term `4` which was present in the second term. The variable `Z` in the second term has been bound to the term `3` which was present in the first term.

The mechanism which the programmer is provided with to ensure there will be no conflicting variable bindings is the "mode declaration". There is a mode declaration associated with each relation of a Parlog program. Each of these *pragmas* is used to express restrictions upon the normal unification algorithm. For every argument of a relation there is a corresponding unification restriction represented in the mode declaration. This is a static annotation interpreted at compile-time. There is one mode declaration per procedure, and the unification restrictions apply globally to the heads of all the relation's clauses. Each argument is annotated as being "input" or "output". If an argument is annotated as being input this means that this argument in a defining clause is not allowed to bind any variables in this argument position in the goal process, but bindings are allowed in the opposite direction i.e. from the call to the head of the defining clause. If an argument is designated as output then bindings are only allowed to flow from the defining clause to the calling goal.

Mode declarations, together with guards, give rise to single bindings of shared variables which do not need to be untrailed because the properties of the mode declaration imply that no guard literal is allowed to bind a variable in the calling goal. If this was allowed and an alternative candidate clause were selected for further reduction then the binding would have to be undone. To implement this untrailing operation could be very costly as some form of multiple environment scheme would be required to store all bindings and record where they were made.

A mode declaration takes the form

```
mode p(m1, m2, ..., mk).
```

where `k` is the number of arguments of the relation `p/k`. An input is designated by the `?` syntax and output by the ↑ syntax. As an example, the mode declaration for the `merge3/4` relation is

```
mode merge3(?, ?, ?, ↑).
```

Its first three arguments are the three lists the relation will try to merge. These are declared as being inputs. The fourth argument, the resulting merged list, is specified as being an output argument.

A process, which is attempting to reduce, must respect the modes of its defined relation. If any of the arguments are marked as being inputs then the process must abide by the above rules. If by instantiating any of its environment's variables the goal process were able to reduce, then it moves into a suspended state pending the instantiation of the relevant variables. If one of these variables is instantiated by a sibling process then the suspended process is woken up and can then make another attempt to reduce.

Other Parlog Syntax and Operational Features

Parlog programs consist of a set of relations. Each relation consists of a set of clauses and an associated mode declaration. Each clause consists of a head, a guard, and a body. Both the guard and body are conjunctions of literals. There are three forms of conjunction in Parlog which can used by the programmer. These are sequential `&`, parallel `//`, and neutral `and`. For example

```
A & B
A // B
A and B
```

In the first case the execution of B can only take place once A has successfully terminated. In the second case the two conjuncts can be executed in parallel if the underlying implementation permits. In the third case the neutral conjunction operator can be safely replaced by either a sequential or parallel conjunction operator. This is preferable if the behaviour of the program remains unaltered whichever operator is chosen. It also allows a compiler to replace neutral operators according to the target architecture on which Parlog is implemented. If the target were a highly-parallel dataflow architecture then it might be feasible to replace neutral conjunctions with their parallel equivalents. In all the above the whole conjunction can only succeed if all of the separate conjuncts succeed.

The clauses that make up a relation are separated by clause search operators. These designate in what order the clauses are to be used for the reduction of a corresponding goal literal. Clauses can be separated by three different sorts of search operator. These are the sequential ;, parallel \\, and neutral "..". For Example

$\texttt{Clause}_1$ \\
$\texttt{Clause}_2$;
$\texttt{Clause}_3$ ..
$\texttt{Clause}_4$.

The final . at the end of $\texttt{Clause}_4$ is the syntax denoting the end of a procedure definition. The above procedure definition is parsed as

;(\\($\texttt{Clause}_1$, $\texttt{Clause}_2$), ..($\texttt{Clause}_3$, $\texttt{Clause}_4$)).

$\texttt{Clause}_1$ and $\texttt{Clause}_2$ are tested for candidacy in parallel. If both of these computations terminate - resulting in both of them being noncandidates - then the next step in the calling process's reduction will depend upon the translation of the neutral search operator. If it has been translated as the parallel version then $\texttt{Clause}_3$ and $\texttt{Clause}_4$ will be tested for candidacy in parallel. If it was transformed to the sequential form then $\texttt{Clause}_3$ is tested for candidacy; only if $\texttt{Clause}_3$ results in it being a noncandidate is $\texttt{Clause}_4$ considered.

Example Programs

Merging Two Lists

The following program merges two input lists and produces the result as output.

```
mode merge(?,?,↑).
merge([U|X], Y,[U|Z]) ← merge(X, Y, Z).
merge(Z, [U|Y], [U|Z]) ← merge(X, Y, Z).
merge([], Y, Y).
merge(X, [], X).
```

The first two input-annotated arguments are the two input lists. Examining each of the four clauses we find that in each case at least one argument is required to be nonvariable in order for the computation to proceed. As soon as there is an element present on any of the two input lists, it is output, and the process iterates with the rest of the corresponding input list. If either one of the input streams should terminate, by being bound to the empty list, the rest of the output becomes the other input stream.

Partitioning a List About An Element

The next example partitions a list into two sublists. One sublist consists of elements less than a given input, the other sublist of elements greater than or equal to the input.

```
mode partition(?,?,↑,↑).
partition(U, [V|X], [V|X1], X2) ←
   less(V, U) :
   partition(U, X, X1, X2).
partition(U, [V|X], X1, [V|X2]) ←
   lesseq(U, V) :
   partition(U, X, X1, X2).
partition(U, [], [], []).
```

There are two inputs; these consist of the list to be partitioned (2nd argument), and the element to partition the list about (1st argument). Examining the clauses we see that a partition process will suspend until the second argument is at least bound to a list constructor. This stops the process becoming ensnared in an infinite recursive computation. The third argument is the list of elements which are less than the given input, tested using the "less than" primitive `less/2`. The fourth argument is the list of elements of the original list which are greater than or equal to the partition element (making use of the "less than or equal" primitive).

Sorting a List

The following program sorts a list into ascending numerical order. It employs the Quicksort method of sorting, [79].

```
mode sort(?, ↑).
sort(List, Sorted) ← qsort(List, Sorted, []).

mode qsort(?, ↑, ?).
qsort([U|X], Sortedh, Sortedt) ←
   partition(U, X, X1, X2),
   qsort(X1, Sortedh, [U|Sorted]),
   qsort(X2, Sorted, Sortedt).
qsort([], Sorted, Sorted).
```

The `sort/2` clause reduces to a call of the quicksort algorithm given by the relation `qsort/3`. The intended meaning of the relation is that the ordered version of the input list is the difference between the second and third arguments of the relation. This is an example of the use of difference lists to concatenate lists in constant time, [29]. To sort a list it is partitioned into two sublists about its first element; one sublist will contain those elements which are strictly less than the first element and the other sublist those elements which are greater than or equal to the first element; quicksort is then recursively applied to these sublists. The sorted list is the sorted version of the first sublist appended to the first element of the original list, which is in turn appended to the sorted version of the second sublist.

Compilation

In this section the part of the compilation process which is common to both of the abstract architectural models proposed in this research is described. The transformation process is that given by S. Gregory, [73], the implementation of which is described by I. Foster in [60].

Transformation into Kernel Parlog

The first stage of compilation consists of the transformation of a source Parlog program into its "Standard Form". The resulting output is known as "Kernel Parlog" or "KP". Consider the source Parlog clause given below.

```
R(t1, ..., tk) ← G : B.
```

The first step in the compilation process is to replace each head argument by a mutually-distinct independent new variable, that is a variable name that is not currently used in the program. A call to the one-way unification primitive, `<=`, described below, is added to the guard for each input argument, and a call to `<=` is added to the body for each of the output arguments. If a variable, say `Q`, is contained in more than one input argument term, then new variables are introduced for each occurrence, `Q1`, ..., `Qj` where `j` is the number of occurrences. Calls to the test unification primitive, `=` (in this case `Q = Q1`, ..., `Q = Qj`) are added to the guard `G` to test that all the values of the variables are identical.

In the clause shown above, suppose that the mode declaration for R specifies that the first i arguments are inputs and the rest of the argument are outputs. The standard form of the clause for R is,

```
R(P1, ..., Pi, Pi+1, ..., Pj) ←
    t1 <= P1, ..., ti <= Pi,
    ⟨test unifications for repeated variables of t1, ... ti⟩,
     G :
     Pi+1 <= ti+1, and ... and Pj <= tj and
     B.
```

The terms t1, ..., ti are the original input argument terms with all but the first occurrence of each variable replaced by new distinct variables. The test unifications are introduced to check the syntactic equality of any repeated variables. All of the additional primitive calls added to the guard are to be executed in parallel with the original source Parlog guard, G. This is because unification is order-independent in Parlog. The output matching calls to <= added to the body can either be executed in parallel, sequentially or in any combination with the original body, B.

The syntax <= denotes the Parlog "one-way unification" primitive. It is used to implement the one-way pattern matching specified by Parlog's unification algorithm. Consider the call,

```
t1 <= t2
```

where t1 and t2 are terms. This call will attempt to unify the two terms by binding variables in t1. If it can succeed by binding variables in t2 then the call suspends. The call will ultimately succeed if, and only if, the t1 and t2 are syntactically identical. If t1 is a variable the call cannot fail unless the "occur check" (a test that no variable is bound to a term containing that same variable) is implemented. Note that the mode of <= is (↑, ?) and it is the only relation that can be called with a non-variable term as an output argument.

A call to the test unification primitive is denoted by =. The mode of which is (? ?). This primitive attempts to unify its two arguments without binding any variables in either argument. The call will suspend if it can proceed by binding a variable in either of the arguments. The call will ultimately succeed, or fail, depending upon whether the arguments are syntactically identical. In a clause's Standard Form every input argument of a call will appear on the right of a call to <=, the left argument of which will be an input term from the head of the source Parlog clause. This explicitly ensures that the input matching requirement will be satisfied. No variables in the caller's environment can be instantiated by any call to <= or = in the guard. This will ensure that the guard computation will not bind any variable in the call, that is it is safe, providing the original source Parlog guard is safe. Every output argument of the original source Parlog clause will appear as the left argument to a call of <= in the body. This will ensure that output matching will only be performed after commitment.

An Example : Transforming The List Partition Relation

As an example of the transformation to Kernel Parlog consider the `partition/4` program given above. Its Kernel Parlog form, after the above transformation is performed, is

```
partition(P1, P2, P3, P4) ←
    [V|X] <= P2, V < P1 :
    P3 <= [V|X1] and
    P4 <= X2 and
    partition(P1, X, X1, X2) ..
partition(P1, P2, P3, P4) ←
    [V|X] <= P2, P1 ≤ V :
    P3 <= X1 and
    P4 <= [V|X2] and
    partition(P1, X, X1, X2) ..
partition(P1, P2, P3, P4) ← [] <= P2 :
    P3 <= [] and
    P4 <= [].
```

All of the original argument terms have been replaced by new variables, `P1`, `P2`, `P3` and `P4`. In the original source version the first argument was an input variable, so adding an input matching call, to the guard, would be pointless. This illustrates the general optimisation of not adding calls to the input matching primitive for those input head arguments which are variables. Calls to <= have been added for the two output arguments in the body of the clauses.

In this example, the resulting Kernel Parlog can be further optimised. In the first clause the call `P4 <= X2` is redundant and `X2` can be replaced by `P4` throughout the clause since `X2` is a variable which will be unbound at the time of the call and is the right argument of an output matching primitive. Also by this optimisation the call to `P3 <= X1` in the second clause is redundant. If a head argument term is a variable and is not contained in an input argument, or any of the guard literals, than there is no need to introduce a call to the matching primitive. The resulting Kernel Parlog is shown below.

```
partition(P1, P2, P3, P4) ←
    [V|X] <= P2, V < P1 :
    P3 <= [V|X1] and
    partition(P1, X, X1, P4) ..
partition(P1, P2, P3, P4) ←
    [V|X] <= P2, P1 ≤ V :
    P4 <= [V|X2] and
    partition(P1, X, P3, X2) ..
partition(P1, P2, P3, P4) ←
    [] <= P2 :
    P3 <= [] and
    P4 <= [].
```

Transformation to KP-And-Or-Tree

Kernel Parlog is architecture-independent but the next stage of the compilation process will introduce some architectural bias. There are two different forms into which Kernel Parlog can be further simplified: "KP-And-Or-Tree" and "KP-And-Tree". KP-And-Or-Tree is an intermediate language suitable for an architecture that directly supports the And-Or control model of Parlog. The KP-And-Tree language supports only And-Parallelism. It is more coarse-grain than KP-And-Or-Tree but makes great use of the metacall control structure (explained later in this chapter).

Any neutral clause search or conjunction operators are also translated into their appropriate forms at this stage. In the Packet-Rewriting model proposed later, all the neutral operators are transformed into their parallel equivalents. This is because the unit of work is itself quite small, and to exploit as much parallelism as possible, while keeping the processing elements busy, it is necessary to have a large quantity of potential work available. In the Multi-Sequential model the operators are replaced by their sequential forms. The unit of work in this model is variable in size and we wish it to be as large as possible to avoid costly process switching. In the implementation of the Multi-Sequential mode it is not necessary to create value cells to hold variables on the heap if they are shared by sequentially separated conjunct processes; the variables can be stored safely in argument registers.

In both the computational models, Packet-Rewriting and Multi-Sequential the chosen target language is KP-And-Or-Tree. This is because KP-And-Or-Tree is Kernel Parlog with the unification matching primitives completely compiled out into simpler forms. It is very much closer to the source form than KP-And-Tree and, therefore, much easier to debug. KP-And-Or-Tree is relatively fine-grained when compared to KP-And-Tree and should match better with the fine-grain model than KP-And-Tree since it is a graph-rewriting model of computation. In addition, the KP-And-Tree model requires a mechanism to suspend processes on sets of variables whereas KP-And-Or-Tree processes will suspend, pending the instantiation of at most one variable. The attachment of a suspended process to a variable is a very simple machine operation. A KP-And-Tree implementation also requires the implementation of a "metacall" facility [73]. This route is not considered a viable option but its merits, related to this research, are discussed at the end of this chapter.

Compilation to KP-And-Or-Tree involves transforming all of the built-in primitives into sets of much simpler procedures. All uses of the matching instruction `<=` are simplified, leaving only calls to the test unification primitive `=` to be implemented (by a recursive procedure). In the Packet-Rewriting model this is compiled into a set of simpler instructions whilst in the Multi-Sequential model it is implemented as a machine instruction. Finally the output is optimised to remove redundant instructions. The conventions used below are that arbitrary terms are represented as `t`, `t1`, ... etc, nonvariable terms by `nt, nt1,` ... etc, constants by `k, k1,` ... etc, and variables by the usual underscore notation.

The compilation of source Parlog to Kernel Parlog introduces calls to <= and = of a certain form. Introduced calls to = will have variables as both arguments. Introduced output matching calls to <= will have a variable as a left argument and introduced input matching calls of <= will have a variables for the right argument. In the case of an output matching call, the left argument will always be a nonvariable term containing no more than one occurrence of each variable. The only form of calls to these primitives which can contain arguments of arbitrary form are those introduced by the programmer into the source Parlog.

If both of the arguments to <= or = are nonvariable terms then it is quite simple to transform them. However, the arguments must be one of the following : the same constant, both be lists, or both be structures having the same functor and arity. The simplifications are :

```
F(t1, ..., tj) <= F(t1, ..., tj)
```

this call is replaced by

```
t1 <= t1, ..., tj <= tj
```

```
[t1|t2] <= [t1|t2]
```

this call can be replaced by

```
t1 <= t1, t2 <= t2
```

```
k <= k
```

this call is removed because the constants will be equal; the empty list, `[]`, is treated as a constant.

As an example consider the following call

```
F(k1, [V1|k2], G(V2), V3) <= F(k1, [[]|V4], V5, V6)
```

is transformed into

```
V1 <= [], k2 <= V4, G(V2) <= V5, V3 <= V6
```

These simplifications can also be applied to the `=` primitive. The simplification process stops when every call to `<=` and `=` has a variable for at least one of its arguments. It is possible to simplify calls of `=` if one of the arguments is a nonvariable, i.e. `nt = V`. If `nt` is ground then it is simplified to `nt <= V`. If `nt` contains variables `V1`, ..., `Vi`, then these are replaced by new variables, `U1`, ..., `Ui`, in `nt` to give a new term `nt` and parallel calls are introduced to match the new variables. These calls to `=` will have variables for both arguments, i.e.

```
nt <= V, U1 = V1, ..., Ui = Vi
```

For calls to `nt <= V` introduced into the source Parlog by the programmer, the calls are transformed so that all of variables in `nt` are distinct. If `nt` contains occurrences of the variable `Q`, then they are replaced by new variables say `Q1`, ..., `Qj` to obtain a new term `nt`, and the call becomes

```
nt <= V, Q = Q1, ..., Q = Qj
```

After applying all of the above transformations the only forms of call to `=` and `<=` are

```
V1 = V2
nt <= V
V <= t
```

The call `nt <= V` must be implemented efficiently since it is introduced for every nonvariable head argument. First of all those calls whose left argument is not a shallow term are transformed. A shallow term is a constant, or a list or structured term whose arguments are variables. If the left argument is a `j`-ary structured term whose first `i` arguments are nonvariable terms and the rest are variables :

```
F(nt1, ..., nti, Vi+1, ..., Vj) <= P
```

the nonvariable terms are replaced by new distinct variables and calls to `<=` are introduced to individually match the variables with their corresponding terms. So in this case the call becomes,

```
F(D1, ..., Di, Vi+1, ..., Vj) <= P and
( nt1 <= D1, ..., nti <= Di )
```

The same transformation is performed in the case of non-shallow list terms as left arguments.

The use of the neutral `and` operator signifies that it is acceptable to attempt the inner matching in parallel with the outer matching. In the Packet-Rewriting model this is the translation performed, since it is guaranteed to execute correctly, because the inner matching cannot proceed until the introduced variables have been instantiated.

The only calls left to be considered are those `nt <= V` with shallow left arguments. There are three forms of shallow term : constants, lists, and structures. Consider constants first :

```
k <= V
```

There are two sequential steps to be performed to do the matching. Firstly, to check that `V` is instantiated and then that it is bound to the constant `k`. This compiles to a sequence of calls to simpler primitives :

```
data(V) & get_constant(k, V)
```

The predicate `data/1` is a primitive which suspends if the argument is an unbound variable. A call to `data/1` never fails and can succeed as soon as the variable is instantiated.

Consider the case where the shallow argument is a list :

```
[V1|V2] <= V
```

First of all `V` is checked to ensure that it is instantiated using a call to `data/1`. `get_list/3` is then called to check that the argument is a list and to split the list into its head and tail components. The `assign/2` primitive is then used to load the extracted head and tail into `V1` and `V2`. The call becomes :

```
data(V) & get_list(V, U1, U2) &
( assign(V1, U1) and assign(V2, U2) )
```

In the case of structured data :

```
F(V1, ..., Vj) <= V
```

a call to `data/1` is performed first to check `V` is instantiated. Using the `get_structure` primitive the bound variable is examined to make sure it is a structured term with functor `F/j`. This will also place the arguments into a set of temporary variables which are loaded into `V1`, ..., `Vj` by a group of `assign/2` primitives :

```
data(V) & get_structure(F/j, V, U1, ..., Uj) &
( assign(V1, U1) and ... and assign(Vj, Uj) )
```

The family of `get_` instructions can be implemented easily since they do not have to check that their arguments are instantiated because of the preceding `data/1` instructions. Also, because of the temporary variables, the output arguments are guaranteed to be uninstantiated variables thus making the primitives even simpler.

The only instruction whose output argument is not guaranteed to be the first occurrence of a variable is `assign/2`. It is possible that the variable in question could have been bound by a sibling process. Thus the first action of `assign/2` is to check that its output argument is unbound. If it is bound a runtime error occurs; if not then the output argument is overwritten by the second input argument term. The occur check, if it is to be implemented, will be done by `assign/2`. If the output argument variable occurs in the input argument term then the occur check will fail.

A call of the form :

```
V <= t
```

will compile to

```
assign(V, t)
```

The test unification primitive = is implemented as a recursive machine code routine in both of the models proposed here. It tests that both arguments are instantiated to the same term. Other source Parlog primitives such as `plus/3` and `times/3` are simplified by using `data/1` primitives to test the state of the input arguments, making the actual primitives easier to implement. For example :

```
t1 < t2
```

becomes

```
( data(t1) and data(t2) ) & less(t1, t2)
```

Primitives with output arguments, compile to code which ends with a set of `assign/2` calls to perform the output. For example :

```
read(V)
```

becomes

```
$read(U) & assign(V, U)
```

The `$read/1` primitive does not check that its argument is a variable. It is simpler to implement than `read/1` because does it not have to execute a complex routine to wake up suspended processes that `read/1` may have to. This task is left to the `assign/2` primitive.

If it happens that in a call to `assign/2`, the output argument is the first occurrence of a variable then the call can be removed, and the variable replaced by the input argument term throughout the clause. This is because the variable is guaranteed to be unbound at the time of the call.

If the input argument is a variable, and it is the first occurrence of it, then the output argument can be replaced throughout the clause by the input argument since it will be unbound at the time of the call

A Note on Using Indexing

In addition to the optimisations described in [73], type testing indexing instructions are also used [175]. These are generated by the KP-And-Or-Tree architecture-specific compiler. They are `switch_on_tag`, `switch_on_constant` and `switch_on_structure`. The `switch_on_tag` instruction branches to different sets of assembly code depending upon the type of a specified argument. It is used to filter out clauses which cannot possibly match, before spawning unification processes for all of a relation's defining clauses. The `switch_on_constant` instruction is only used if there are corresponding input arguments of more than one clause which are different constants. Its arguments are the designated input argument and a table of code labels. A hash function, applied to the input argument, is used to compute an index into the table. At the entry computed, is the address of the assembler code for the clause with that constant. The `switch_on_structure` is used similarly but the hash function is applied to function symbols.

Chosen Dialect

The dialect of Parlog used in this research is the one described in [73], but without the "metacall" facilities for the reasons given below. The `set/3` and `subset/3` primitives are simply escape routines which Parlog programmers can use to obtain "all-solutions" to sets of Prolog clauses. An interpretive implementation in Parlog is described in [31]. An alternative method is to invoke a Prolog machine with the query to carry out the deduction as a separate coroutine [33]; in other words, boot a Prolog machine, virtual or real, and passing over the all-solutions query for it to solve by backtracking through all of the solutions. This is the method prescribed here, as it is likely to be the most efficient method, since the Prolog clauses can be compiled to WAM code. By doing this there is the possibility of having a single architecture that can run both Parlog and Prolog, two separate machines, or some combination lying in between these two extremes.

It should also be mentioned that the programs used to evaluate the two models, Packet-Rewriting and Multi-Sequential, were small since the bulk of the research centred around the design and implementation of the models. This left little time to devote to the development of suitable compilers and meant that all executable program images were hand-compiled.

The language as described in [73] proposes the use of a metacall facility. There are several variants, of which the three argument version is the most powerful needed to be considered here. The format of the `call/3` is given below :

```
mode call(?, ↑, ?).
call(Proc, Status, Control).
```

The first argument `Proc` is a term denoting a relation call. In the mechanism described here this would be compiled into a WAM instruction to be passed over to an invoked Prolog machine. In logic programming architectures it is usual to pass arguments from goal clause code to procedure code in "argument registers". In the Parlog architectures presented here, and in the SPM, the set of argument registers ("a-registers") is often referred to as if it was a single entity, an "argument vector" ("a-vector"). The a-vector registers corresponding to the arguments having to be copied over to the argument registers of the Prolog machine by `put_value/2` instructions. The second argument represents the current execution status of the call. This is one of three states : `succeeded`, `failed` or `stopped`. The third argument is used to control the active call by binding the variable to a term, or to an incomplete list whose head is one of `stop`, `continue` or `suspend`.

There are semantic problems associated with the metacall as specified in [73]. This is the so-called "anti-substitutability" problem. This arises because a metacall can never fail (the `Status` argument is used to relay failure information). The semantics of the metacall allows bindings to be exported out of the metacall. Because of this two resolvants having exactly the same declarative semantics can produce different results. For instance consider the following two resolvants :

```
← call(X=0, _, _), call(X=1, _, _).
```

and

```
← call(X=0, _, _), X = Y, call(Y=1, _, _).
```

The first process system will succeed whereas the second will fail. GHC has a metacall facility with sound anti-substitutability properties [170]. Further work is needed on the semantics of process invocation in Parlog before the metacall with communication is adopted. In this work "metainterpretation" to implement metacalls as used in the Logix system [78] [147] [159], where an interpreter is enhanced with the extra features required by the programmer and is then used to partially evaluate the program to execute, resulting in an suitably enhanced program [9] [56] [64] [83] [92] [133].

Chapter 3 A Fine-Grain Graph-Reduction Model of Computation

Introduction

Functional languages are similar to logic programming languages in that they are both declarative. Thus an investigation of whether a computational model which has proved successful for the implementation of functional languages could be enhanced to support Parlog. The result of this work is the Packet-Rewriting computational model and the construction of an emulator for the model (described in chapter 4). In this chapter we present an overview of the Parlog-independent part of the Packet-Rewriting computational model.

The Alvey FLAGSHIP project [49] [72] [119] [137] [148] [178] [179] is centred around the building of a packet-based parallel computer architecture that has graph reduction (described below) as its computational model. In this chapter the Flagship model, of September 1985 [177] is described. During the course of the research described here the model has been enhanced to enable features such as manipulation of arbitrary data structures to be used. General constructor and selector functions have been added to enable the use of richer functional languages such as Hope+ [116] and Miranda [167], and to support other programming languages.

In order to allow programming language implementors more freedom, thus making their job easier, some of the lower level features that were implicitly present in the original computational model have been raised to the Compiler Target Language (CTL) level in the work described in this chapter and chapter 4. These features include assignment (overwriting of program graph) and copying pieces of code graph. This also allows a machine code programmer to use these aspects for the purposes of optimization.

The operational semantics of the model has its roots in graph reduction. One of the desirable consequences of this is that it enables shared computation to be realised. Each equation of a declarative program can be thought of as a template specifying a rewriting operation. If a term in the current resolvant matches the left hand side of an equation, the root of the subgraph corresponding to the term is overwritten by the graph representing the right-hand side of the rule. Each node of the function graph is represented abstractly by a packet, and reduction is carried out on those packets that have been demanded for evaluation. In a more concrete model, packets will contain a number of fields and several nodes may be represented in a single packet.

Graph Reduction

It is possible to represent each equation of a declarative program as a graph. The first step in this transformation is to translate all of the function definitions into curried form. For example the equation

```
f(x, y) = (x + y) * (x - y)
```

becomes

```
f(x, y) = * (+ x y) (- x y)
```

All equations are now of the form : operator applied to a set of operands. The corresponding graph and its packet form is shown below

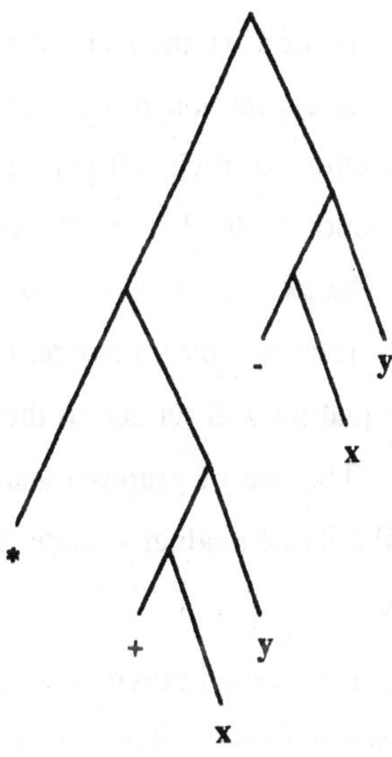

Figure 1. *Example graph representation of function.*

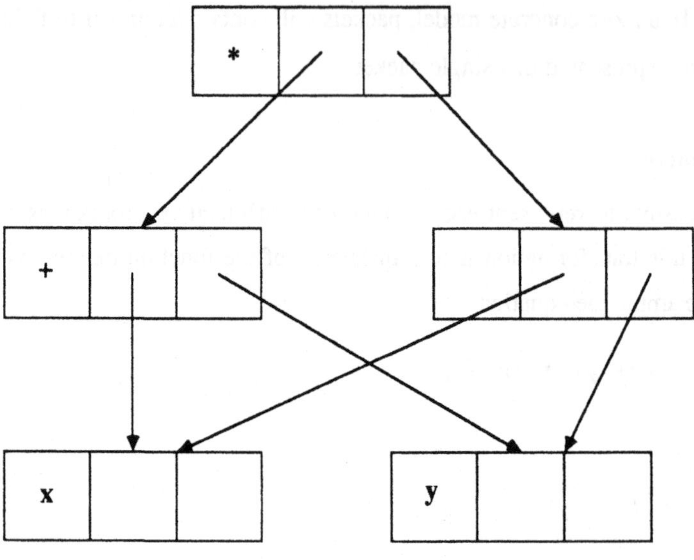

Figure 2. *Example packet representation of function.*

The leaves of the graph are either functions or their argument terms. The leftmost leaf is always the outermost function in the expression represented by the graph. The internal nodes of the graph represent applications of their left subgraph to their right subgraph. In the above example the leftmost function symbol is `*`. Its two arguments are the two subgraphs `(+ x y)` and `(- x y)`. The two terms `x` and `y` appear more than once in the equation. Functional languages are referentially transparent which means all occurrences of the same symbol within in an equation will reduce to the same values if and only if it is possible to fully evaluate them. The use of graphs means that it is possible to share common subgraphs, and terms will only be evaluated once. Thus in the above example `x` and `y` will be evaluated only once.

A graph is evaluated using a process known as *graph reduction*. The process attempts to reduce a graph (the function to be evaluated), with the aid of any programmer equations provided (the program), into a form which cannot be reduced further (a canonical form). At any stage of the reduction there may be many nodes that can be reduced. A computation rule must be provided in order for a graph reduction system to choose its redexes (those roots of subgraphs which can be reduced). The computation rule which is of interest here is "normal order reduction". A graph reducer, using a normal order computation rule, always chooses the outermost redex. In the graph representation this is always the leftmost leaf of the graph. If there is a canonical form then a normal order reducer is guaranteed to find it.

A pure normal-order graph reducer will in general not exploit any parallelism that is available in a program. It will only reduce one node of the graph at a time. It is possible at compile time however to analyse a program and, using knowledge of the semantics of the programming language, discover opportunities where parallelism may be explored.

For instance, in the example given, there is initially only one redex, the graph associated with * and its two arguments. In order for this graph to be reducible, the two arguments of * must be reduced until they are of integer form. In a pure normal-order reduction system, the outermost redex is always chosen. Thus the first argument of * will be fully evaluated, then only after this has completed will reduction of its second argument be attempted. The function * is "strict" in both its arguments. That is, if reduction of any of the arguments does not terminate then the reduction of the * term will fail to terminate. Thus both of the arguments could in fact be evaluated safely in parallel if the rightmost argument does not contain side-effects that must be executed after operations executed in the leftmost argument. In this case the execution of the rightmost argument must be suspended until it can be executed safely. The model proposed here allows for any parallelism detected by strictness analysis at compile-time to be exploited at run-time.

The Computational Model

The model of computation consists of two parts: the packet store and the pool of processing elements. Associated with each packet is a unique identifier to distinguish it from others in the packet pool; in a more concrete implementation this would be implicit as the packet's address. Packets can be thought of as processes (actors) which communicate with each other via messages. These messages are also realised as packets in the abstract model. The packet pool is made up of two distinct sorts of packet: active packets and inactive packets.

Active packets occur as a result of a demand for the reduction of an inactive packet. Processing elements poll the packet pool for active packets. These will be rewritten according to their definition, as given by the program, and the packets comprising the right-hand side of the matching equation written back to the packet pool. In the model, the right-hand side of an equation is also held in packet form because the model seeks to preserve the declarative code-data equivalence at the computational model level making it simple to construct code at runtime such as in the case of meta-interpretation. This is unlike the Alice architecture [41] [42] which makes a clear distinction between code and data at the computational model level, leading in turn to great difficulties in implementing those features of languages which treat code and data as though they were the same (e.g. database predicates in Prolog).

Nature of Packets

In the model, the two sorts of packet, active and inactive, may be in one of three states: rewritable, dormant, or blocked. The active ones may be either rewritable or blocked, whilst an inactive packet will only be in the dormant state. A dormant packet is one which is currently not being considered for rewriting by a processor. A rewritable packet is one that a processor is attempting to reduce to a set of new packets. A blocked packet is one which had been a candidate for rewriting but lacked sufficient information for the reduction to proceed.

The processing agents will poll the pool of packets for those which are in the rewritable state, much the same as in the Alice model [41] [42]. Packets can either be addressed by state, such as described above for rewritable packets, or by address e.g. to obtain free packet identifiers when writing back right-hand side packets.

Packet Structure

There are seven major components of a packet. These are listed as follows:

(a) **Packet Identifier**

These are unique integers used by processing elements to refer to particular packets. Packet identifiers are not necessary in the emulation of the model, nor in a more concrete form of implementation, since the normal memory addressing scheme is used wherein the packets are referred to by their addresses (a word of memory is a packet in this case).

(b) **Packet Type**

This packet component distinguishes between the various types of packet. In the case of declarative programming languages only two types need to be supported: the ghost and non-ghost types. Packets which are of type ghost are used to inform a processing element that a piece of computation, it is empowered to perform, is being executed elsewhere.

(c) **Suspended Count**

This states how many values are pending for a packet before it can be made rewritable. An active packet may require information about its arguments before it can be reduced. A function may require that its argument is a constructor, but its present form is that of a dormant call to a function returning the required constructor. In situations such as this, the packet will move into the blocked state, and will activate those arguments for which it requires more information. For each argument activation which returns, the suspended count is decremented. Only when the suspended count is zero does the packet become rewritable once more and a processing element resumes trying to reduce it.

(d) **Garbage Collection**

This can be used to implement either a reference count, or a marker for a mark-scan method of storage reclamation. In the current emulation this field is present but unused.

(e) **Packet Context**

This is used to state properties which are relevant to a specific packet. These include strictness information and information about sharing. In all the emulations performed, only strictness information was considered. It is usually the job of the programming language compiler to generate this information on a per packet basis. An example is in the code for an equation where the function in question is always strict in a particular argument. It is possible that code could be generated at runtime to call this function. If this call is to execute correctly then the strictness information for that function would have to be stored somewhere, whereas, if it is held in the packets making up the equation, then no lookup is required.

(f) **Fields**

Each node of a graph contains references to its subgraphs. Associated with each term is an outermost symbol. This can either be a constructor or a rewritable function. In the graph these will be the leftmost leaves of any branch. In order to keep packets a fixed size, thus making storage easier, there must be a limit placed upon the length of leftmost branches in the graph. These leftmost branches are known as spines. By restricting the number of arguments a term can have (one less than the number of fields in a packet) the length of a spine can be at most this number. The first major field of a packet is a leaf at the end of a spine. The other major fields represent the right branches of the spine.

(g) **Return Address**

A packet which does not represent a normal form of a term, in the domain of packets, will be a candidate for reduction. A packet requiring the normal form of another packet will issue a request to have it evaluated. The eventual result of this evaluation must be returned to the now suspended caller. In order to accomplish this, the return address field is used to indicate to which packet the eventual value of this packet must be returned.

Operational Semantics of the Model

In general the first field of a packet will either be a pointer to another packet, or it will be a built-in operation of the model. Examples of built-in operations are predicates such as `get_list/3` and functions such as `head`. If it is a pointer to a packet then the packet containing the pointer is treated as a call to the packet it is referencing. The other fields of the packet are the arguments of the call to the referenced code graph. If the packet's first field is a function value then this is the special case of a call where the function can be represented in a single field. Pointer type fields are the physical representation of the arcs in the abstract code graph. Typically a pointer as a first field will represent a function name in an actual program.

There are basic field types to cope with all the sorts of objects which are built into the model. These are integer, real, character, boolean, null and nil constructor value fields. To simulate beta-reduction (the rewriting of the left-hand side of an equation by its right-hand side) there is a special type of field called an argument selector. A field of this type indicates which argument of the calling packet should be substituted *in situ* in this field. The other type of field is a return address which enables sharing of computation to be achieved.

It is often the case that a referenced packet is not in its completely evaluated normal form. On such occasions it is necessary to put to sleep (alter its state to blocked) the rewritable packet. The blocked packet will be woken up only when the referenced packet is a value and then it will attempt to rewrite itself. To achieve this the blocked packet needs to know how many values are pending before it can become rewritable. This is implemented by having a "suspended pending values" count for each packet. This is initially zero but is incremented for every packet which is not in the correct form, as pointed to by one of its fields when this packet has been fired. In order to send a wake up signal to the suspended packet, the fired packet needs to know the destination of its eventual value. To implement this each packet has a return address attached which is either null, or consists of a packet address of the sleeping packet, and a field number in which to substitute its value.

Strictness information about built-in operations is made available by having an argument descriptor attached to each function value field. This indicates which of the packet's fields are in use and also shows if the function is strict or non-strict in a particular argument. There is one indicator for each field of the packet and therefore for every argument of the function.

Strictness information obtained and generated by compilers is accommodated using a packet context field in each packet. This will indicate whether a particular field of a packet is used or unused. It also shows whether a packet referenced by a particular field should be fired before attempting the call operation on the packet referenced by its first field. Thus if a user-defined function is analysed and found to be strict on a particular argument then the appropriate packet context of the calling packet for that function will have a strict indicator for that field embedded in it.

In the physical representation a packet denotes the node of a graph. A pointer field in a packet, a node of the graph, indicates the presence of a subgraph attached to the node. Because a graph is a representation of the right hand side of an equation, other packets in the graph which must be evaluated, besides the one referenced by the caller, might require access to the caller's arguments. To cater for this, each pointer field has a pointer context as well as an address. This pointer context consists of an array of indicators, one for each field of the calling packet. Each one indicates whether the referenced subgraph requires that field of the caller to enable beta reduction of the equation to take place. In other words whether a subgraph requires to be executed in the same calling context, hence the name pointer context.

Sharing of Computation

In order to share results of computations, a second type of packet is introduced called a ghost. The presence of a ghost packet, as a node of the graph, indicates that the value for the packet that used to be at that node is being computed. A ghost packet tells an accessing packet, in effect, to "go to sleep, tell me who you are and I will wake you up when I have a value for you". On accessing and activating a referenced packet, it has to be decided whether this further computation can possibly be shared. If it can, a copy of the referenced packet is taken, activated, and a ghost packet is left *in situ* at that reference. A packet which has all the context it requires for evaluation is in a position to be shared. That is to say, all its pointer context fields must be of null context (i.e. they do not have any context) and the packet must not contain any argument selectors.

A rewritable packet suspends whenever it accesses a ghost packet. It then adds its address to a null field of the ghost packet, along with an indication of which field it requires the eventual value to return to. When a packet in the evaluated state attempts to return its value to a waiting packet, it first checks to see if it is a ghost. If it is not then the returning packet substitutes its value, as given by the field number of its return address, in the usual way.

If the packet the value is being returned to is a ghost, then the active packet takes a copy of the ghost and overwrites the original with a copy of itself (the value), thus enabling subsequent accesses to refer to the result of the computation. Should the value packet consist of a single field then, before overwriting the ghost, the value packet has to be converted into a rewritable packet. This is done so that chains of pointers will not build up (which would in itself mean the implementation of "intelligent" selector functions that would have to follow arbitrarily long reference links until a constructor is found). To overcome this effect the single field value is augmented by an indirection constructor function in the first field and the original first field being moved into the new packet's second field. This packet is used to overwrite the ghost instead of the original. An indirection operator simply returns the value of its second field. On encountering an indirection packet, a selector will suspend and then activate the packet. This cycle will keep going until the selector references its appropriate constructor.

The value packet then creates a copy of itself with a return address equal to the return address of the ghost (the original activating packet). It then inspects the ghost packet for non-null fields. These must be of the type "return address value" otherwise an implementation error has occurred. For each return address value field encountered it creates a copy of itself. Each of these copies will be in the evaluated state, possessing a return address equal to the non-null field, thus being in a position to wake up all packets that will have been suspended pending the eventual value of the original packet.

The implementation described above is satisfactory for most cases. However, the number of packets that can suspend, pending the value of a single computation, is limited by the number of null fields in a virgin ghost packet. There are two solutions to this problem; the first is to attempt to build some form of data structure instead of the usual ghost packet. Alternatively, when the ghost packet is full, a way must be provided of creating a new copy of the original packet. If the number of suspended packets only occasionally exceeds the number of free fields in a ghost then the second solution might be acceptable. Nevertheless, in general the former solution seems to be preferable.

Packet Description Language

The language used to describe packets to the emulator of the Packet-Rewriting model is based on a Prolog-like syntax. Packets are represented as terms whose principle functor is `p/n` where `n` is the number of components, which is itself determined by the number of major fields per packet. The first argument is used to express three different kinds of information. It denotes if a packet is active, fully evaluated, or, if neither of these is the case, then its address is displayed. The possible terms are `act`, `val` and `addr(A)`, where `A` denotes the address of a packet (the packet identifier). The second argument of a packet term is used to denote the type of the packet. The only types which need supporting are ghost, `gh`, and nonghost, `ngh`. The "suspended pending values" count is the next argument and is simply an integer in the range zero to the number of fields per packet minus one. Next follows the garbage collection field which is used for reference counting and consists of an integer in the range zero up to the maximum number of possible references that a packet can have possibly have pointing to it. Theoretically, this number can, of course, be the size of the whole packet store but in practice it will be an implementation-dependent constant. The garbage collection argument of the packet term will be denoted by the anonymous variable symbol _ since it is not considered here. Next is the packet context which is itself represented by a term. The principal functor of this term is `pconx/n` where `n` is the number of major fields in a packet. The only displayed information is strictness and whether the field contains any useful information. The two strictness indicator symbols are `s` for strict and `n` for non-strict. If the field in question is unused then the anonymous variable symbol _ is used to denote this fact.

A field can be a pointer, an argument selector, or a value of some form. A pointer field is indicated by having a term with principal functor `ptr/2`. The first argument of `ptr/2` will be the address of the referenced packet. The second argument of a `ptr/2` term contains the context of the pointer which is denoted, in the packet term, by a sub-term `ptrconx/n`, where `n` is the number of major fields in a packet. A null context is denoted by the anonymous variable _. For each field of the calling packet which is required by the subgraph given by the pointer, the atom `rqd` is used. The argument number of any `rqd` atoms corresponds to the number of the field required by the sub-graph. Thus the term `ptr(2,ptrconx(rqd, rqd, _, _, _)` indicates a reference to the packet at address two and that both the subgraph given by the referenced packet and the subgraph below it require the first and second arguments of the calling packet.

An argument selector type field is indicated by the presence of a term `argsel(N)` as the first character in the field, where `N` is the number of the field to be substituted *in situ.* Therefore `argsel(3)` in a field means "substitute the third field of the calling packet in here".

The other type of field, a value field, is denoted by the term `val/1`. An integer value field is denoted by the term `int/1`, where the argument is the integer itself. Similarly reals are denoted by the term `real/1`, where the argument is the real number. The denotation of a character is a term `char/1` whose argument is the ascii equivalent of the character in decimal. A null value field is signified by the term `null/0`, and a nil value field by the term `nil/0`. A boolean field is indicated by a term `bool/1`, with an argument `true` or `false`. A return address value field is indicated by the term `raddr/2`; its two arguments are the address and the field number to which it must return a value.

The only other type of value field is a function value given by the term `fun/2`. Its first argument is the mnemonic representing the function. Its second is the function's argument descriptor, represented by the term `argdes/n`, where `n` is one less than the number of fields allowed per packet; this is because the function value takes up one of them. Typical mnemonics are `add` for the addition function and `ite`, standing for if-then-else, for the conditional operator. An argument descriptor contains one symbol for each possible argument. The symbol `_` denotes that argument field of the function is unused, `s` denotes that the function is strict on that argument field, and `n` denotes non-strictness.

The last component of the packet is always its special return address field and is represented in exactly the same way as a return address value field, i.e. with an `raddr/2` term.

An Example

```
f(x)  <=  (x * x) + (x * x)
```

The corresponding code for the above equation is given below. The notation `raddr(_, _)` in a packet indicates a null return address.

```
p(addr(1), ngh, 0, _, pconx(s,s,s,_,_), val(fun(add, argdes(s,s,_,_))),
ptr(2,ptrconx(_,rqd,_,_,_)), ptr(2,ptrconx(_,rqd,_,_,_)), val(null),
val(null), raddr(_,_)).

p(addr(2), ngh, 0, _, pconx(s,s,s,_,_), val(fun(mul, argdes(s,s,_,_))),
argsel(2), argsel(2), val(null), val(null), raddr(_,_)).
```

The code packet for the call f(3) is also shown below. The notation raddr(A,F) is the return address of the sleeping packet that demanded the value of f(3), A is the address and F is the field number.

```
p(act, ngh, 0, _, pconx(s,s,_,_,_), ptr(1,ptrconx(_,_,_,_)),
val(int(3)), val(null), val(null), val(null), raddr(A,F)).
```

The packet at address 1 has non-null pointer context fields. Note that these are designated as strict by its packet context. Therefore the first step in the evaluation is to create a new demand packet. Only one is created in this case because the fields in question are identical. All of the fields of the calling packet have been used by the referenced packet and so it can be dispensed with and the packet at 1 made active. This gives us the following situation.

```
p(act, ngh, 0, _, pconx(s,s,s,_,_), val(fun(add,argdes(s,s,_,_))),
ptr(3,ptrconx(_,_,_,_)), ptr(3,ptrconx(_,_,_,_)), val(null),
val(null), raddr(A,F)).

p(addr(2), ngh, 0, _, pconx(s,s,_,_,_), ptr(2,ptrconx(_,_,_,_)),
val(int(3)), val(null), val(null), val(null), raddr(_,_)).

p(addr(2), ngh, 0, _, pconx(s,s,s,_,_), val(fun(mul, argdes(s,s,_,_))),
argsel(2), argsel(2), val(null), val(null), raddr(_,_)).
```

The active packet now has pointer values present in fields designated as strict by its packet context. This active packet will be suspended pending the value of these two fields. One of the demands for the value of the packet, at address 3, must arrive at the packet before the other. In this case assume it is the one given by the demand for the value of the second field. This demand will see that the packet at 3 can be shared and so will create a copy, make it active, and leave a ghost packet *in situ*. This situation is depicted below

```
p(addr(4), ngh, 2, _, pconx(s,s,s,_,_), val(fun(add,argdes(s,s,_,_))),
val(null), val(null), val(null), val(null), raddr(A,F)).

p(act, ngh, 0, _, pconx(s,_,_,_,_), ptr(3,ptrconx(_,_,_,_,_)), val(null),
val(null), val(null), val(null), raddr(4,3)).

p(addr(4), gh, 0, _, pconx(_,_,_,_,_), val(null), val(null), val(null),
val(null), val(null), raddr(4,2)).

p(act, ngh, 0, _, pconx(s,s,_,_,_), ptr(2,ptrconx(_,_,_,_,_)), val(int(3)),
val(null), val(null), val(null), raddr(3,1)).

p(addr(2), ngh, 0, _, pconx(s,s,s,_,_), val(fun(mul,argdes(s,s,_,_))),
argsel(2), argsel(2), val(null), val(null), raddr(_,_)).
```

There will be an attempt to rewrite the two active packets in parallel if possible. Consider the active packet with the single non-null field first. This is a demand for the value of the packet stored at address 3. On inspection the active packet sees that the referenced packet is a ghost indicating that the value is already being computed. The active packet is a simple demand and hence leaves its return address in the first free field in the ghost. The other active packet inspects the packet at 2 and, finding that it contains argument selector fields, replaces those relevant fields *in situ*. All of the fields of the active packet have now been used and so a copy of the updated packet at 2 is made active, having a return address equal to that of the original active packet. The situation now is depicted below

```
p(addr(4), ngh, 2, _, pconx(s,s,s,_,_), val(fun(add,argdes(s,s,_,_))),
val(null), val(null), val(null), val(null), raddr(F,A)).

p(addr(3), gh, 0, _, pconx(n,_,_,_,_), val(raddr(4,3)), val(null),
val(null), val(null), val(null), raddr(4,2)).

p(act, ngh, 0, _, pconx(s,s,s,_,_), val(fun(mul,argdes(s,s,_,_))),
val(int(3)), val(int(3)), val(null), val(null), raddr(3,1)).
```

The active packet is now in a form where it can be rewritten. The fields designated as strict by the packet's context are, in this case, the same as those which are designated as strict by the argument descriptor of the `mul` operator. The situation after the rewrite is shown below.

```
p(addr(4), ngh, 2, _, pconx(s,s,s,_,_), val(fun(add,argdes(s,s,_,_))),
val(null), val(null), val(null), val(null), raddr(F,A)).

p(addr(3), gh, 0, _, pconx(n,_,_,_,_), val(raddr(4,3)), val(null),
val(null), val(null), val(null), raddr(4,2)).

p(val, ngh, 0, _, pconx(s,_,_,_,_), val(int(9)), val(null), val(null),
val(null), val(null), raddr(3,1)).
```

The packet to which the value packet is trying to return is inspected and found to be a ghost. A copy of the ghost packet, augmented by an indirection operator, is taken and this value packet is substituted *in situ* for the ghost thus enabling any further demands to access the value. A copy of the value packet is then made for the return address field and each non-null return address value field of the ghost:

```
p(addr(4), ngh, 2, _, pconx(s,s,s,_,_), val(fun(add,argdes(s,s,_,_))),
val(null), val(null), val(null), val(null), raddr(F,A)).

p(val, ngh, 0, _, pconx(s,_,_,_,_), val(int(9)), val(null), val(null),
val(null), val(null), raddr(4,2)).

p(val, ngh, 0, _, pconx(s,_,_,_,_), val(int(9)), val(null), val(null),
val(null), val(null), raddr(4,3)).

p(addr(3), ngh, 0, _, pconx(s,s,_,_,_), val(fun(ind,argdes(n,_,_,_,_))),
val(int(9)), val(null), val(null), val(null), raddr(_,_)).
```

The two value packets then substitute their values *in situ,* as given by their return address fields. As each substitution takes place the "suspended pending values" count of the blocked packet is decremented. When the two value packets have been dealt with the count is zero and so the packet can be reactivated giving

```
p(act, ngh, 0, _, pconx(s,s,s,_,_), val(fun(add,argdes(s,s,_,_))),
val(int(9)), val(int(9)), val(null), val(null), raddr(F,A)).
```

This packet can be rewritten to give the final result of the computation, `f(3)` as shown below

```
p(val, ngh, 0, _, pconx(s,_,_,_,_), val(int(18)), val(null), val(null),
val(null), val(null), raddr(F,A)).
```

Selectors and Constructors

In order to allow general constructors and selectors, as in Hope+ and Miranda, it will be necessary to have a flag to indicate when a function is a constructor or not. A general selector mechanism, as shown below, is also used. This is an addition to the original

Flagship model. The second field indicates which field of the referenced packet is required and the reference is given in the third field. The fourth field indicates the form the first field of the referenced packet should be in if it is a constructor.

```
p(_, ngh, 0, _, pconx(s,s,n,s,_), val(fun(sel,argdes(s,n,s,_))),
val(int(FieldNumber)), ptr(PktAddr,ptrconx(_)), val(fun(Fun,ArgDes)),
val(null), raddr(_,_)).
```

Remarks on the Model of Computation

The computational model is simple but very flexible. It is thus a good candidate for being realised in hardware in order to obtain experience with declarative architectures. The software for such an architecture will be written in a purely declarative style. This means a declarative language which incorporates notions of concurrency will have to be supported at the implementation level. Languages for this purpose have been designed such as Parlog, Concurrent Prolog and GHC. The implementation of the most promising of these, Parlog, will be the subject of chapter 4.

Note that no account of any garbage collection mechanism has been described so far because it is not clear at present which method will eventually be used. As it stands the model would be very inefficient but to alleviate this problem blocks of the code graph can be copied where possible instead of a single packet at a time (providing it is safe to do so, i.e. they do not contain any shared code). Also partial evaluation could be used at compile-time to eliminate unnecessary run-time computation.

Chapter 4 Implementing Parlog On A Packet-Rewriting Computational Model

Introduction

The model described in the previous chapter is based upon incremental packet copying; that is the model will make copies of packets which are being interpreted as code whenever it needs to do so. This preserves the property of there being no distinction between code and data at the implementation level; it is this single factor which most influences the design choices that have to be made during implementation.

The basic unit of the implementation is the Parlog relation; each relation being compiled down to a set of packets. In the functional language implementation, it is the case that the only set of packets that need copying for any function are those for the equation whose left hand side matches the redex term. Parlog is a programming language based upon committed-choice nondeterminism. Because of this several equations for the same relation could match and thus have their guards computed. It is desirable to avoid an initial copying of packets for any guard computations that will eventually fail. The incremental packet-copying model enables this to be accomplished, which is an advance over the Alice KP-And-Or-Tree implementation [31] [61] [73]. In reality only the packets of the successfully committed-to clause need copying but the identity of this clause is undecidable. Thus copying packets whose evaluation does not contribute to the final answer cannot be avoided; but in our implementation, the minimal amount of packets are copied to compute the needed result. This issue is discussed in more detail in chapter 6.

The Implementation

Representing Variables

One normally encounters two types of entity in the first field of a packet (referred to as the operation field). These are rewritable and constructor functions. Rewritable operations correspond to user-defined functions and built-in basic operations of the architecture. Constructor functions are used to represent data structures and give rise to an obvious method of representing variables; define a new constructor function `var` and refer to such packets as "variable packets". Since a variable packet can never be a candidate for reduction, and the constructor `var` has no arguments, the argument descriptor will contain unused indicators, namely _ , for every other field apart from the operation field in the packet. In the Parlog implementation only five fields are needed so there are four such indicators: `argdes(_,_,_,_)`. Variable packets are allowed to be overwritten. This is to allow variables to become bound to terms when executing unification primitives.

Binding Environments

In general, for each clause in a relation, it is necessary to create a corresponding new binding environment, the components of which are all of the clause's local variables and any call environment variables the clause process may bind. On commitment to a candidate clause its environment is then made public, enabling any sibling conjunction processes to see any bindings made by this clause process. This is equivalent to the `environ own, commit own,` sequence of instructions in the SPM [60]. A clause process will take a copy of the set of packets which represents this environment as it requires them. It was decided that an environment should take the form of a list of packets, since this is a simple dynamically alterable structure. The packets that represent a template of the environment need to be distributed throughout the clause processes for a relation, but each clause process then makes its own copy of the environment. This procedure enables variable packets to be copied only when required; it is not desirable to make copies of variables for each clause only to find individual clause processes failing and the copies not being used.

As there is no distinction between code and data at the packet level, if further action is not taken then a clause process will simply make use of the template packets for binding operations instead of their clones (the template packets are constructors and not rewritable and thus would not be copied, as required, to create a separate binding environment for each clause that needed one). This is because the packets are in constructor form, i.e. contain a constructor function in their operation field, and so are regarded as fully evaluated in the graph-reduction model. Thus if no further action is taken the packets representing the binding environment will be copied and shared between all the clauses which can lead to binding conflicts.

The Copy-Packet Primitive

To solve this problem, a copy-packet primitive, `cpp`, is incorporated into the basic instruction set. For each packet denoting a variable, a `cpp` packet is introduced *in-situ* into the binding environment list which then references the original variable packet. The binding environment now consists of a list of reference packets, each one pointing to a variable packet. When a `cpp` packet is encountered at execution time, a copy of the referenced packet is made and the value returned is a packet containing a reference to this newly created packet. This operation is illustrated graphically below.

The sequence :

```
p(act, ngh, 0, _, pconx(s,n,_,_,_), val(fun(cpp,argdes(n,_,_,_))),
ptr(1,ptrconx(_,_,_,_,_)), val(null), val(null), val(null),
raddr(A,F)).

p(addr(1), ngh, 0, _, pconx(_,_,_,_,_), val(null), val(null),
val(null), val(null), val(null), raddr(_,_)).
```

results in the following set of packets being produced

```
p(val, ngh, 0, _, pconx(n,_,_,_,_), ptr(2,ptrconx(_,_,_,_,_)),
val(null), val(null), val(null), val(null), raddr(A,F)).

p(addr(2), ngh, 0, _, pconx(_,_,_,_,_), val(null), val(null),
val(null), val(null), val(null), raddr(_,_)).
```

Diagrammatically this operation looks like :-

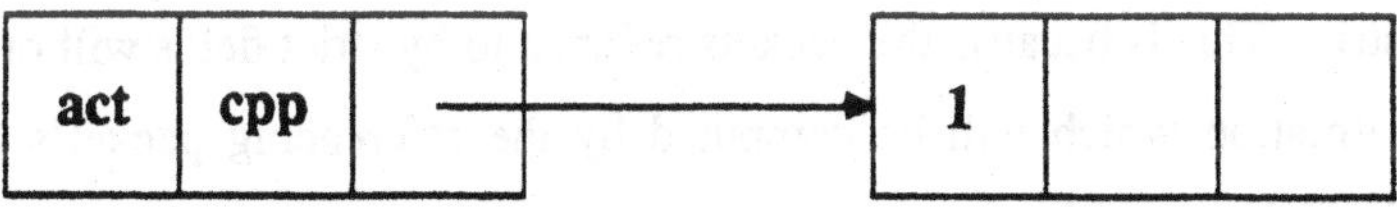

Figure 3. *Copy packet primitive before execution.*

which then results in

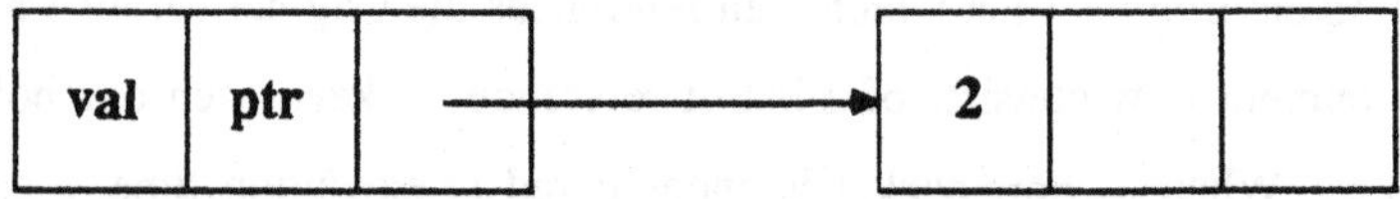

Figure 4. *Copy packet primitive after execution.*

Solving the Strictness Information Conflict

In the initial functional language architecture, fields can only be designated as strict or non-strict. If a field is designated as strict in the packet context, and the field contains a reference to a packet which does not contain a constructor in its main operation field, then the referenced packet is to be repeatedly fired until either it is a value or it references a constructor packet. This idea conflicts with a notion of a `cpp` packet which requires only one initial activation and then any returned reference is to be ignored until further notice. This problem arises because logic programming enables programmers to instantiate variables to terms which contain variables, this does not occur in the functional programming paradigm. To overcome this problem, a strictness indicator which lies between being fully strict and lazy is used. This indicator enables a field to be fired once and then become non-strict. The notation `o`, meaning "once" , is used to express this. It should be noted that a packet with a first field, which is of pointer type, will return a reference to itself when fired.

An ordering has now been introduced upon the use of any strictness information in a packet. Those fields that are designated as having a fire-once strictness are fired first and the packet awaits the result of all of these activations before attempting to deal with any fields that are strict. This is because the packets referred to by strict fields will often want to refer to information which will be computed by the referencing packet's fire-once fields. In pseudo-C the algorithm is :-

```
Packet P ;
PacketAddress A, NewA ;
```

```
FieldNumber i ;
Bool PacketLocked ;
Bool FireOncePresent ;
Bool StrictPresent ;
A = get_active_packet_address() ;
P = read_packet_from_store(A) ;
PacketLocked = UNLOCKED ;
FireOncePresent = FALSE ;
StrictPresent = FALSE
NewA = get_free_packet_identifier() ;
for ( i = FirstFieldIndex ; i <= LastFieldIndex ; i++ )
  {
   if ( (P.pconx[i].usage == USED) &&
        (P.pconx[i].strictness == FIRE_ONCE) &&
        (P.MajorFields[i].type == PTR) )
    {
     if ( PacketLocked == UNLOCKED )
      {
       lock_packet(NewA) ;
       PacketLocked = LOCKED ;
      }
     FireOncePresent = TRUE ;
     P.SuspendedCount++ ;
     P.pconx[i].strictness = NON_STRICT ;
     activate(P.MajorFields[i].ptr.ref) ;
    }
  }
if ( FireOncePresent == TRUE )
 {
  write_packet_to_store(NewA,P) ;
  unlock_packet(NewA) ;
 }
else
 {
  for ( i = FirstFieldIndex ; i <= LastFieldIndex ; i++ )
   {
    if ( (P.pconx[i].usage == USED) &&
         (P.pconx[i].strictness == STRICT) &&
         (P.MajorFields[i].type == PTR) )
     {
```

```
      if ( PacketLocked == UNLOCKED )
       {
        lock_packet(NewA) ;
        PacketLocked = LOCKED ;
       }
      StrictPresent = TRUE ;
      P.SuspendedCount++ ;
      activate(P.MajorFields[i].ptr.ref) ;
     }
  }
 if ( StrictPresent == TRUE )
  {
   write_packet_to_store(NewA,P) ;
   unlock_packet(NewA) ;
  }
}
evaluate_no_pconx_packet(P) ;
```

The type of locks used are blocking and atomic. If a process tries unsuccessfully to acquire a lock then it suspends. Processes that release locks on packets wake all processes that are sleeping on that lock, the newly awoken processes will then compete for the lock.

The first action the emulated packet agent performs is to get the address of an active packet via the `get_active_packet_address()` routine. The agent then gets this relevant packet from store. When this packet has been dealt with, a new free packet address is requested in order to write back the processed packet. The agent then inspects the packet context. For each indicator that is "fire once" and the corresponding field is of pointer type, the referenced packet is fired and the indicator is set to "non strict". The "suspended pending values" count is incremented for each such "fire once" indicator. If this is necessary, the original packet has to be locked before activating any referenced packets. The locking has to be performed because the activated packets might return values before the original packet has been processed. If this happens, there is the possibility of having two inconsistent versions of the same packet at the same time. After going through the indicators in turn, the next step depends upon whether any "fire once" references were present. If there were, then the packet is written back to store at a new address and the packet unlocked. If no "fire once" indicators were present, the packet is inspected for "strict" reference fields. If there are any of these present then the packet is locked, the referenced packets are activated and for each one of these the original packet's "suspended pending values" count is incremented. The updated packet is then written back to store and unlocked. If the packet context of an active packet is fully dealt with then the packet can be evaluated without regard to its context. This is the routine `evaluate_no_pconx_packet/1`.

All packets having a field that references a `cpp` packet will have their appropriate strictness indicator marked as `o`. The packet will see the fire-once indicator and examine the corresponding field. If this is a reference then it will fire the referenced packet and then change its strictness indicator to non-strict: `n`. If the referenced packet was a `cpp` packet , the referencing packet will copy the packet it points to and return a value packet containing its address. This will be inserted into the original field, i.e. the original `o` designated field. The original packet now has indicator `n` so reduction can now proceed as normal. The computation sequence for a set of packets involving the use of a fire-once strictness indicator is depicted below where `add` is the integer addition primitive. Integers are represented in this model using the integer constructor `int`.

```
p(act, ngh, 0, _, pconx(s,s,o,_,_), val(fun(add,argdes(s,s,_,_))),
ptr(1,ptrconx(_,_,_,_,_)), ptr(2,ptrconx(_,_,_,_,_)), val(null),
val(null), raddr(A,F)).

p(addr(1), ngh, 0, _, pconx(s,n,_,_,_), val(int(2)), val(null),
val(null), val(null), val(null), raddr(A,F)).

p(addr(2), ngh, 0, _, pconx(s,n,_,_,_), val(int(3)), val(null),
val(null), val(null), val(null), raddr(A,F)).
```

after a number of computation steps we obtain

```
p(act, ngh, 0, _, pconx(s,s,n,_,_), val(fun(add,argdes(s,s,_,_))),
ptr(1,ptrconx(_,_,_,_,_)), val(int(3)), val(null), val(null),
raddr(A,F)).

p(addr(1), ngh, 0, _, pconx(s,n,_,_,_), val(int(2)), val(null),
```

```
val(null), val(null), val(null), raddr(A,F)).
```

Using the Copy-Packet Primitive to Implement Binding Environments

Binding environments are represented in the implementation as lists. The environment for a two element set of variables is shown here.

```
p(addr(1), ngh, 0, _, pconx(s,o,n,_,_), val(fun(cons,argdes(n,n,_,_))),
ptr(2,ptrconx(_,_,_,_)), ptr(3,ptrconx(_,_,_,_)), val(null),
val(null), raddr(_,_)).

p(addr(2), ngh, 0, _, pconx(s,n,_,_,_), val(fun(cpp,argdes(n,_,_,_))),
ptr(4,ptrconx(_,_,_,_)), val(null), val(null), val(null), raddr(_,_)).

p(addr(3), ngh, 0, _, pconx(s,o,n,_,_), val(fun(cons,argdes(n,n,_,_))),
ptr(5,ptrconx(_,_,_,_)), val(nil), val(null), val(null), raddr(_,_)).

p(addr(4), ngh, 0, _, pconx(s,_,_,_,_), val(fun(var,argdes(_,_,_,_))),
val(null), val(null), val(null), val(null), raddr(_,_)).

p(addr(5), ngh, 0, _, pconx(s,n,_,_,_), val(fun(cpp,argdes(s,n,_,_))),
ptr(6,ptrconx(_,_,_,_)), val(null), val(null), val(null),
raddr(_,_)).

p(addr(6), ngh, 0, _, pconx(s,_,_,_,_), val(fun(var,argdes(_,_,_,_))),
val(null), val(null), val(null), val(null), raddr(_,_)).
```

For reasons of clarity two variable packets are depicted, at addresses `4` and `6`, one for each variable in the source Parlog. In the code generated by the compiler, only one such variable packet will in fact be present, this is because it is the *copies* which are used for binding, the compiler-generated packet is used merely as a template. Notice the `cpp` packet which serves to create a new instance of the variable when it is fired. To look up the binding of a variable, the address of its environment is used together with the knowledge of which element it is. The example below shows the set of packets representing a typical guard, in this case the formula `[1, 2] <= X`. This one-way unification primitive, <=, will attempt to unify its right hand side with the list on its left hand side. If the term on the right-hand side is a variable then the <= packet will suspend, pending the variable's instantiation. The packet designated as active by the `act` first subterm is the call packet. The packets rooted at address `4` produce a copy of the local variable `X`. The packets rooted at address `5` represent the term `[1,2]`.

```
p(act, ngh, 0, _, pconx(s,n,n,_,_), val(fun(<=,argdes(n,n,_,_))),
ptr(5,ptrconx(_,_,_,_,_)), ptr(4,ptrconx(_,_,_,_,_)), val(null),
val(null), raddr(A,F)).

p(addr(1), ngh, 0, _, val(fun(cons,argdes(n,n,_,_))),
ptr(2,ptrconx(_,_,_,_,_)), val(nil), val(null),
val(null), raddr(_,_)).

p(addr(2), ngh, 0, _, pconx(s,n,_,_,_), val(fun(cpp,argdes(n,_,_,_))),
ptr(3,ptrconx(_,_,_,_)), val(null), val(null), val(null), raddr(_,_)).

p(addr(3), ngh, 0, _, pconx(s,_,_,_,_), val(fun(var,argdes(_,_,_,_))),
val(null), val(null), val(null), val(null), raddr(_,_)).

p(addr(4), ngh, 0, _, pconx(s,n,_,_,_),
val(fun(head,argdes(n,_,_,_,_))), ptr(1,ptrconx(_,_,_,_)),
val(null), val(null), val(null), raddr(_,_)).

p(addr(5), ngh, 0, _, pconx(s,s,n,_,_), val(fun(cons,argdes(n,n,_,_))),
val(int(1)), ptr(6,ptrconx(_,_,_,_,_)), val(null), val(null),
val(null), raddr(_,_)).

p(addr(6), ngh, 0, _, pconx(s,s,s,_,_), val(fun(cons,argdes(n,n,_,_))),
val(int(2)), val(nil), val(null), val(null), radd(_,_)).
```

Implementing Suspension-On-Variable

In the sequential implementation of Parlog, the SPM, a blocked process is attached to a suspension list associated with the unbound variable whose instantiation it is awaiting. In the Packet-Rewriting model, a process (unit of work) is a packet. The method needed to accomplish the suspension list management is already provided for by the ghost mechanism; although it is used for a slightly different concept, it behaves in the manner required. If a packet needs one of its arguments to be instantiated and it is in fact a variable, i.e. contains a variable constructor, the packet will move into the suspended state. The now blocked packet's "suspended pending arguments" count is incremented and its address in the packet store is inserted into the variable packet along with the number of the argument in question. Together these two pieces of information enable the now suspended packet to be re-activated later.

A process that instantiates a variable will first take a local copy of the variable packet before overwriting it with the binding. It will then inspect the local copy and for each non-null field, excluding the field containing the variable constructor, decrement the suspended count of the specified blocked packet. If the suspended count is zero, the blocked packet is then reawakened and moves into the active state. The set of fields containing the addresses of the suspended packets mirrors the suspension list of the SPM. If there are more suspended packets than fields in the variable packet then the last field in the variable packet references other packets which contain the rest of the chain.

A list is used because it is a simple structure. In the previous example there was only one variable involved, the right-hand side of <=, so the binding environment list had only one element. In this case there was no need to resort to a list structure and a head selector. The corresponding simplified set of packets is shown below.

```
p(act, ngh, 0, _, pconx(s,n,n,_,_), val(fun(<=,argdes(n,n,_,_))),
ptr(3,ptrconx(_,_,_,_)), ptr(1,ptrconx(_,_,_,_,_)), val(null),
val(null), raddr(A,F)).

p(addr(1), ngh, 0, _, pconx(s,n,_,_,_), val(fun(cpp,argdes(n,_,_,_))),
ptr(2,ptrconx(_,_,_,_,_)), val(null), val(null), val(null), raddr(_,_)).

p(addr(2), ngh, 0, _, pconx(s,_,_,_,_), val(fun(var,argdes(_,_,_,_))),
val(null), val(null), val(null), val(null), raddr(_,_)).

p(addr(3), ngh, 0, _, pconx(s,s,n,_,_), val(fun(cons,argdes(n,n,_,_))),
val(int(1)), ptr(4,ptrconx(_,_,_,_)), val(null), val(null), raddr(_,_)).
```

```
p(addr(4), ngh, 0, _, pconx(s,s,s,_,_), val(fun(cons,argdes(n,n,_,_))),
val(int(2)), val(nil), val(null), val(null), raddr(_,_)).
```

Program Output

What exactly is the output of a query ? Is it a recognition of whether it is a logical consequence of the program, or, what is normally the programmer's intention, is it the bindings of the variables present in the query ? As in the case of most Prolog implementations both output-interpretations are given by compiling inline a set of output function packets, one for each variable, along with the packets generated for the query. The primitive output function provided is the Parlog encoding of the Prolog predicate `write/1`, the user output procedure is the `print_term/1` routine supplied with the SPM system.

Representing Predicates

A Parlog procedure consists of a set of clauses. To represent the fact that the elements of the set belong to the same relation, the code (a set of packets) is stored using three-element constructor packets in a similar way to that of using two-element constructor packets to store lists. Literals of the current resolvent are separated by conjunction operators. The same principle is applied here, a three-element constructor packet is used to structure the goals. The type of constructor depends upon the type of operator involved. Clauses are combined using `or` packets, and literals with `and` packets. The format of both these constructor packets is shown below.

```
p(_, ngh, 0, pconx(s,s,n,s,_), val(fun(or,argdes(s,n,s,_))),
val(int(I)), ptr(C,ptrconx(_,_,_,_,_)), val(bool(Commit)),
val(null), raddr(_,_)).

p(_, ngh, 0, pconx(s,s,n,s,_), val(fun(and,argdes(s,n,s,_))),
val(int(I)), ptr(C,ptrconx(_,_,_,_,_)), val(bool(Fail)),
val(null), raddr(_,_)).
```

The second major field of the `or` and `and` packets is used to hold a count of the number of clauses or literals in relevant packet set (`I` in the above). For `or` packets, `I` is the number of possible clauses that might produce a candidate clause process. This enables the `or` packet to be able to tell when it should fail, i.e. if the count should become zero, and there are no more untried clauses, then the call has failed. In the case of `and` packets this information is used by the packet to indicate when it should succeed. It is a count of the number of currently active literal processes plus the number of dormant conjunction literal processes. When this is zero then all of the conjuncts have succeeded and therefore the whole conjunction can succeed. The actual literals and clauses are held in another list-like structure. The third major field of an `or` or `and` packet is a reference to this structure. The fourth field in each case is used as a flag, hence the `bool` constructor. In the case of the `or` packet this is used during the commitment mechanism; for `and` packets this is used to indicate the result of the conjunction.

An `or` or `and` packet when fired will activate each packet in its process list referenced by its third argument. A clause process is represented using a clause-process constructor, `clause`. The packet format is given below.

```
p(_, ngh, 0, _, pconx(s,s,o,_,n), val(fun(clause,argdes(s,n,n,n))),
ptr(_1,ptrconx(_,_,_,_,_)), ptr(_2,ptrconx(_,_,_,_,_)),
ptr(_3,ptrconx(_,_,_,_,_)), ptr(_4,ptrconx(_,_,_,_,_)), raddr(_,_)).
```

The second major field of a `clause` packet is a reference to the set of packets representing the guard conjunction, `_1`, for the clause in question. The third field contains a reference to the binding environment construction packets, `_2`, for this clause. The fourth field references the packets that make up the body of the clause, `_3`. It is usually the case that the body packets should only be copied for the successfully chosen candidate. The final major field is used to insert the `clause` packet into the chain of clause-process constructor packets and is the constant `nil` or a pointer to the next clause, `_4`.

Both the `and` and `or` packets can be regarded as being a mechanism that behaves like a metacall facility for each process in the `clause` list. The fourth field in `and` and `or` packets can be regarded as a global control variable for these metacalls. In the case of an `or` packet, its first child `clause` packet that has a successfully terminating guard becomes a candidate. It then attempts to instantiate, i.e. overwrite, the fourth field to a representation of the Parlog constant `stopped` (represented as `bool(false)` in the implementation of the model). This will stop any other active `clause` packets from committing. The fourth field acts as though it were a read-only variable once it has been bound. For `and` packets the fourth field indicates whether it can fail (one of its child `clause` packets has failed), or it can succeed (all of its child `clause` packets have succeeded).

In both the cases of `or` and `and` packets, if a child `clause` packet informs its parent that it has succeeded it must also identify itself to its parent packet. The usual way is by including a self-reference in some field of the returned value packet. For clause process packets this enables the corresponding committed `clause` packet to be fired and the set of packets making up the clause's body to be incrementally copied. The identifier of the successful `clause` packet is stored in the first free field of the value packet. The identity of this field is easily recognised by inspecting the format of the packet.

Initially the indicator corresponding to the body reference in the packet context field of a `clause` packet is marked "unused", _. Upon successful commitment of the clause process, this indicator is toggled to "used", denoted by `s`, since its value is now required. An active `clause` packet can thus find out if it has committed by seeing if it is allowed to use its body packets. If the indicator, on this inspection, is "unused" and the packet's guard is successful, the packet will try to commit by informing its parent.

An `or` packet, which has a child `clause` packet that has succeeded, must check the current instantiation of its control variable. If the child packet has failed however, the parent packet will decrement the count of the currently active clauses. If this count is now zero then the call has failed and the `or` packet is overwritten with a "failed" constructor packet of the form `fun(failed,argdes(_,_,_,_))`. The parent of the `or` packet is then sent a "failed" packet as the value of the call. As previously mentioned, a body of a clause is only fired upon commitment. This means that the strictness indicator in the packet context field is "unused" and "strict", thus ensuring that the body reference is fired when its indicator is toggled to "used".

An `and` packet having a child goal `clause` packet that succeeds, will decrement its count of currently active conjunction goals. If this count becomes zero then the whole conjunction is successful. The `and` packet will be overwritten by a "succeeded" constructor packet and a "succeeded" packet is returned as the value of the conjunction to the parent of the `and` packet. The succeeded constructor is `fun(succeeded,argdes(_,_,_,_))`. If one of the child `clause` packets fails, then the parent `and` packet is overwritten with a "failed" constructor packet, the control variable is set to "stopped", and a "failed" packet is sent as the value of the conjunction to the parent of the `and` packet.

Queries

Initially a goal clause is given to the system to prove. This is in the form of a conjunction of goal literals. In packet form this is an `and` packet together with a chain of `clause` packets, one for each goal literal in the goal clause. There is also a set of output packets included to print out the eventual value of the variables. If a variable is uninstantiated then the address of the variable packet is used to identify it uniquely.

The Killing Mechanism

In order to be able to kill off unwanted computations it is necessary to know the locations of all the currently active packets for those computations. When firing a referenced child packet, and if the referenced packet is copied, then the reference field in the original parent packet is overwritten with a reference to this copied packet. To kill off an active packet it is simply unreferenced; this method relies on having a high-priority garbage-collection process to clear up the dereferenced active packets.

Sequential Conjunctions

To implement the sequential conjunction operator `&` it is treated as if it were a conditional function, as shown below.

```
p(_, ngh, 0, _, pconx(s,s,n,s,_), val(fun(ite,argdes(s,n,n,_))),
ptr(_1,ptrconx(_,_,_,_)), ptr(_2,ptrconx(_,_,_,_)),
val(fun(fail,argdes(_,_,_,_))), val(null), raddr(_,_)).
```

The source Parlog formula `T1 & T2` is transformed into "if `T1` then `T2` else fail". This in turn means the number of built-in operations will not unnecessarily increase. If the emulated processing element were realised in hardware then this would help to keep the architecture simple; if the emulated processing element is microcoded, then the amount of microcode will be kept as small as possible; if it is a hardwired architecture, then the finite-state automata upon which it is based will be kept as simple as possible.

General Unification

The equality unification primitive = is not considered to be a basic operation provided by the machine. It is encoded as an operation built up from other simpler operations. The packet structure for the = operation is shown below.

```
p(act, ngh, 0, _, pconx(s,n,n,_,_), ptr(1,ptrconx(_,_,_,_,_)),
ptr(_1,ptrconx(_,_,_,_,_)), ptr(_2,ptrconx(_,_,_,_,_)),
val(null), val(null), raddr(A,F)).

p(addr(1), ngh, 0, _, pconx(s,s,n,n,_), val(fun(ite,argdes(s,n,n,_),)),
ptr(2,ptrconx(_,rqd,rqd,_,_)), ptr(4,ptrconx(_,rqd,rqd,_,_)),
ptr(5,ptrconx(_,rqd,rqd,_,_)), val(null), raddr(_,_)).

p(addr(2), ngh, 0, _, pconx(s,s,s,_,_), val(fun(land,argdes(s,s,_,_))),
ptr(3,ptrconx(_,rqd,_,_,_)), ptr(3,ptrconx(_,_,rqd,_,_)), val(null),
val(null), raddr(_,_)).

p(addr(3), ngh, 0, _, pconx(s,n,_,_,_), val(fun(isvar,argdes(n,_,_,_))),
argsel(2), val(null), val(null), val(null), raddr(_,_)).

p(addr(4), ngh, 0, _, pconx(s,n,n,_,_), val(fun(eqref,argdes(n,n,_,_))),
argsel(2), argsel(3), val(null), val(null), raddr(_,_)).

p(addr(5), ngh, 0, _, pconx(s,s,n,n,_), val(fun(ite,argdes(s,n,n,_))),
ptr(6,ptrconx(_,rqd,rqd,_,_)), ptr(8,ptrconx(_,rqd,rqd,_,_)),
val(bool(false)), val(null), raddr(_,_)).

p(addr(6), ngh, 0, _, pconx(s,s,s,_,_), val(fun(land,argdes(s,s,_,_))),
ptr(7,ptrconx(_,rqd,_,_,_)), ptr(7,ptrconx(_,_,rqd,_,_)), val(null),
val(null), raddr(_,_)).
```

```
p(addr(7), ngh, 0, _, pconx(s,n,_,_,_), val(fun(data,argdes(n,_,_,_))),
argsel(2), val(null), val(null), val(null), raddr(_,_)).

p(addr(8), ngh, 0, _, pconx(s,s,n,n,_), val(fun(ite,argdes(s,n,n,_))),
ptr(9,ptrconx(_,rqd,rqd,_,_)), val(bool(true)),
ptr(10,ptrconx(_,rqd,rqd,_,_)), val(null), raddr(_,_)).

p(addr(9), ngh, 0, _, pconx(s,n,n,_,_), val(fun(eqcon,argdes(n,n,_,_))),
argsel(2), argsel(3), val(null), val(null), raddr(_,_)).

p(addr(10), ngh, 0, _, pconx(s,s,n,n,_), val(fun(ite,argdes(s,n,n,_))),
ptr(11,ptrconx(_,rqd,rqd,_,_)), ptr(12,ptrconx(_,rqd,rqd,_,_)),
val(bool(false)), val(null), raddr(_,_)).

p(addr(11), ngh, 0, _, pconx(s,n,n,_,_),
val(fun(eqfunc,argdes(n,n,_,_))), argsel(2), argsel(3), val(null),
val(null), raddr(_,_)).

p(addr(12), ngh, 0, _, pconx(s,s,s,_,_), val(fun(land,argdes(s,s,_,_))),
ptr(13,ptrconx(_,rqd,rqd,_,_)), ptr(15,ptrconx(_,rqd,rqd,_,_)),
val(null), val(null), raddr(_,_)).

p(addr(13), ngh, 0, _, pconx(s,n,n,_,_), ptr(1,ptrconx(_,_,_,_,_)),
ptr(14,ptrconx(_,rqd,_,_,_)), ptr(14,ptrconx(_,_,rqd,_,_)),
val(null), val(null), raddr(_,_)).

p(addr(14), ngh, 0, _, pconx(s,s,n,_,_), val(fun(cfpd,argdes(s,n,_,_))),
val(int(2)), argsel(2), val(null), val(null), raddr(_,_)).

p(addr(15), ngh, 0, _, pconx(s,s,s,_,_), val(fun(land,argdes(s,s,_,_))),
ptr(16,ptrconx(_,rqd,rqd,_,_)), ptr(18,ptrconx(_,rqd,rqd,_,_)),
val(null), val(null), raddr(_,_)).

p(addr(16), ngh, 0, _, pconx(s,n,n,_,_), ptr(1,ptrconx(_,_,_,_,_)),
ptr(17,ptrconx(_,rqd,_,_,_)), ptr(17,ptrconx(_,_,rqd,_,_)),
val(null), val(null), raddr(_,_)).

p(addr(17), ngh, 0, _, pconx(s,s,n,_,_), val(fun(cfpd,argdes(s,n,_,_))),
```

```
val(int(3)), argsel(2), val(null), val(null), raddr(_,_)).

p(addr(18), ngh, 0, _, pconx(s,s,s,_,_), val(fun(land,argdes(s,s,_,_))),
ptr(19,ptrconx(_,rqd,rqd,_,_)), ptr(21,ptrconx(_,rqd,rqd,_,_)),
val(null), val(null), raddr(_,_)).

p(addr(19), ngh, 0, _, pconx(s,n,n,_,_), ptr(1,ptrconx(_,_,_,_,_)),
ptr(20,ptrconx(_,rqd,_,_,_)), ptr(20,ptrconx(_,_,rqd,_,_)),
val(null), val(null), raddr(_,_)).

p(addr(20), ngh, 0, _, pconx(s,s,n,_,_), val(fun(cfpd,argdes(s,n,_,_))),
val(int(4)), argsel(2), val(null), val(null), raddr(_,_)).

p(addr(21), ngh, 0, _, pconx(s,n,n,_,_), ptr(1,ptrconx(_,_,_,_,_)),
ptr(22,ptrconx(_,rqd,_,_,_)), ptr(22,ptrconx(_,_,rqd,_,_)),
val(null), val(null), raddr(_,_)).

p(addr(22), ngh, 0, _, pconx(s,s,n,_,_),
val(fun(cfpd,argdes(s,n,_,_))), val(int(5)), argsel(2), val(null),
val(null), raddr(_,_)).
```

The subgraph of packets rooted at address `8` in the graph is the rewrite rule for testing instantiated terms to see if they are equal. If the arguments of `=` are both constants, they are then tested to see if they are equal (the packet at `9`). If the arguments are compound terms then first of all a check is made to see if the functors of the two terms are equal (the packet at `11`), if so the processing element calls the `=` recursively for each subterm of the compound term (the subgraph rooted at address `12`).

The `eqref` primitive tests if all of its fields, which are references, are equal. These fields are identified using the strictness indicator for the operator. The operator `eqcon` tests if its designated fields in its containing packet are all constants and are all equal values. The `cpfd` function is the copyfield primitive. Its containing packet's third major field contains a reference to the packet to extract a field from and the second major field contains information as to which field it is.

One-Way Unification

Uses of the one-way unification primitive can be transformed into a sequence of simpler instructions. Consider the atomic formula `2 <= X`. This will be transformed into the equivalent expression `data(X) & get_constant(2, X)`. Using the conditional form of `&` this is coded as the set of packets shown below.

```
p(addr(1), ngh, 0, _, pconx(s,s,n,s,_), val(fun(ite,argdes(s,n,n,_))),
ptr(2,ptrconx(_,reqd,_,_,_)), ptr(3,ptrconx(_,rqd,_,_,_)),
val(bool(false)), val(null), raddr(_,_)).

p(addr(2), ngh, 0, _, pconx(s,n,_,_,_), val(fun(data,argdes(n,_,_,_))),
argsel(2), val(null), val(null), val(null), raddr(_,_)).

p(addr(3), ngh, 0, _, pconx(s,s,s,_,_),
val(fun(get_constant,argdes(s,s,_,_))), val(int(2)), argsel(2),
val(null), val(null), raddr(_,_)).
```

An Example : Input Matching Against a List

Consider the atomic formula `[V1|V2] <= V`. This will be transformed into the equivalent expression `data(V) & get_list(V, U1, U2) & ( assign(V1, U1), assign(V2, U2) )`. The generated set of code packets is shown below.

```
p(act, ngh, 0, _, pconx(s,n,n,_,_), ptr(1,ptrconx(_,_,_,_)),
ptr(_1,ptrconx(_,_,_,_)), ptr(17,ptrconx(_,_,_,_)),
val(null), val(null), raddr(A,F)).

p(addr(1), ngh, 0, _, pconx(s,s,n,s,_), val(fun(ite,argdes(s,n,n,_))),
ptr(2,ptrconx(_,rqd,_,_,_)), ptr(3,ptrconx(_,rqd,rqd,_,_)),
val(bool(false)), val(null), raddr(_,_)).

p(addr(2), ngh, 0, _, pconx(s,n,_,_,_), val(fun(data,argdes(n,_,_,_))),
argsel(2), val(null), val(null), val(null), raddr(_,_)).
```

```
p(addr(3), ngh, 0, _, pconx(s,o,_,_,_), ptr(9,ptrconx(_,_,_,_,_)),
argsel(2), ptr(4,ptrconx(_,_,_,_,_)), argsel(3), val(null),
raddr(_,_)).

p(addr(4), ngh, 0, _, pconx(s,n,_,_,_), val(fun(cpp,argdes(n,_,_,_))),
ptr(5,ptrconx(_,_,_,_,_)), val(null), val(null), val(null), raddr(_,_)).

p(addr(5), ngh, 0, _, pconx(s,o,n,_,_), val(fun(cons,argdes(n,n,_,_))),
ptr(6,ptrconx(_,_,_,_,_)), ptr(8,ptrconx(_,_,_,_,_)), val(null),
val(null), raddr(_,_)).

p(addr(6), ngh, 0, _, pconx(s,n,_,_,_), val(fun(cpp,argdes(n,_,_,_))),
ptr(7,ptrconx(_,_,_,_,_)), val(null), val(null), val(null),
raddr(_,_)).

p(addr(7), ngh, 0, _, pconx(s,_,_,_,_), val(fun(var,argdes(_,_,_,_,_))),
val(null), val(null), val(null), val(null), raddr(_,_)).

p(addr(8), ngh, 0, _, pconx(s,o,n,_,_), val(fun(cons,argdes(n,n,_,_))),
ptr(6,ptrconx(_,_,_,_,_)), val(nil), val(null), val(null), raddr(_,_)).

p(addr(9), ngh, 0, _, pconx(s,s,n,s,_), val(fun(ite,argdes(s,n,n,_))),
ptr(10,ptrconx(_,rqd,rqd,_,_)), ptr(14,ptrconx(_,_,rqd,rqd,_)),
val(bool(false)), val(null), raddr(_,_)).

p(addr(10), ngh, 0, _, pconx(s,n,o,o,_),
val(fun(get_list,argdes(n,n,n,_))), argsel(2),
ptr(11,ptrconx(_,_,rqd,_,_)), ptr(12,ptrconx(_,_,rqd,_,_)),
val(null), raddr(_,_)).

p(addr(11), ngh, 0, _, pconx(s,n,_,_,_), val(fun(head,argdes(n,_,_,_))),
argsel(2), val(null), val(null), val(null), raddr(_,_)).

p(addr(12), ngh, 0, _, pconx(s,n,_,_,_), val(fun(head,argdes(n,_,_,_))),
ptr(13,ptrconx(_,rqd,_,_,_)), val(null), val(null), val(null),
raddr(_,_)).

p(addr(13), ngh, 0, _, pconx(s,n,_,_,_), val(fun(tail,argdes(n,_,_,_))),
```

```
argsel(2), val(null), val(null), val(null), raddr(_,_)).

p(addr(14), ngh, 0, _, pconx(s,s,s,_,_), val(fun(land,argdes(s,s,_,_))),
ptr(15,ptrconx(_,rqd,rqd,_,_)), ptr(16,ptrconx(_,rqd,rqd,_,_)),
val(null), val(null), raddr(_,_)).

p(addr(15), ngh, 0, _, pconx(s,n,n,_,_),
val(fun(assign,argdes(n,n,_,_))), ptr(11,ptrconx(_,rqd,_,_,_)),
ptr(11,ptrconx(_,_,rqd,_,_)), val(null), val(null), raddr(_,_)).

p(addr(16), ngh, 0, _, pconx(s,n,n,_,_),
val(fun(assign,argdes(n,n,_,_))), ptr(12,ptrconx(_,rqd,_,_,_)),
ptr(12,ptrconx(_,_,rqd,_,_)), val(null), val(null), raddr(_,_)).

p(addr(17), ngh, 0, _, pconx(s,n,n,_,_), val(fun(cons,argdes(n,n,_,_))),
ptr(18,ptrconx(_,_,_,_,_)), ptr(20,ptrconx(_,_,_,_,_)), val(null),
val(null), raddr(_,_)).

p(addr(18), ngh, 0, _, pconx(s,n,_,_,_), val(fun(cpp,argdes(n,_,_,_))),
ptr(19,ptrconx(_,_,_,_,_)), val(null), val(null), val(null),
raddr(_,_)).

p(addr(19), ngh, 0, _, pconx(s,_,_,_,_), val(fun(var,argdes(_,_,_,_))),
val(null), val(null), val(null), val(null), raddr(_,_)).

p(addr(20), ngh, 0, _, pconx(s,n,n,_,_),
val(fun(cons,argdes(n,n,_,_))), ptr(18,ptrconx(_,_,_,_,_)),
val(nil), val(null), val(null), raddr(_,_)).
```

The packet with first argument `act`, is the active call to the one-way unifier primitive. The set of packets at addresses `17, 18, 19`, and `20` create the local variables `U1` and `U2`. The call and representation of the `data` primitive is denoted by packets at `1` and `2`. The creation of the variables `V1` and `V2`, used to destruct the list into its head and tail, are created by firing packets at `4, 5, 6, 7`, and `8`. The call of the `get_list` primitive operation is represented by the packets at `10, 11, 12`, and `13`. The `get_list` packet has three arguments, the order of which corresponds to the order of arguments in the Kernel Parlog. The first argument is the input list, and the second and third arguments are the head and tail of the list respectively. The parallel tail-fork of `assign` goals is represented by the packets at `14`, `15`, and `16`. Note that in this example, separate sets of packets to create the variables `U1`, `U2`, `V1`, and `V2` have been used. This has been done only for clarity and in practice a more compact form would be generated.

A More Complex Example : Input Matching Against a Structure

As another example consider the decomposition of a structure, for instance

```
f(V1, V2, V3) <= V
```

The equivalent Kernel Parlog is

```
data(V) & get_structure(f/3, V, U1, U2, U3) &
( assign(V1, U1), assign(V2, U2), assign(V3, U3) )'
```

The generated set of code packets for this expression is shown below.

```
p(act, ngh, 0, _, pconx(s,n,n,_,_), ptr(1,ptrconx(_,_,_,_,_)),
ptr(_1,ptrconx(_,_,_,_,_)), ptr(23,ptrconx(_,_,_,_,_)), val(null),
val(null), raddr(_,_)).

p(addr(1), ngh, 0, _, pconx(s,s,n,s,_), val(fun(ite,argdes(s,n,n,_))),
ptr(2,ptrconx(_,rqd,_,_,_)), ptr(3,ptrconx(_,rqd,rqd,_,_)),
val(bool(false)), val(null), raddr(_,_)).

p(addr(2), ngh, 0, _, pconx(s,n,_,_,_), val(fun(data,argdes(n,_,_,_))),
argsel(2), val(null), val(null), val(null), raddr(_,_)).

p(addr(3), ngh, 0, _, pconx(s,o,_,_,_), ptr(9,ptrconx(_,_,_,_,_)),
argsel(2), ptr(4,ptrconx(_,_,_,_,_)), argsel(3), val(null),
raddr(_,_)).

p(addr(4), ngh, 0, _, pconx(s,n,_,_,_), val(fun(cpp,argdes(n,_,_,_))),
ptr(5,ptrconx(_,_,_,_,_)), val(null), val(null), val(null), raddr(_,_)).

p(addr(5), ngh, 0, _, pconx(s,o,n,_,_), val(fun(cons,argdes(n,n,_,_))),
```

```
ptr(6,ptrconx(_,_,_,_,_)), ptr(22,ptrconx(_,_,_,_,_)), val(null),
val(null), raddr(_,_)).

p(addr(6), ngh, 0, _, pconx(s,n,_,_,_), val(fun(cpp,argdes(n,_,_,_))),
ptr(7,ptrconx(_,_,_,_,_)), val(null), val(null), val(null),
raddr(_,_)).

p(addr(7), ngh, 0, _, pconx(s,_,_,_,_), val(fun(var,argdes(_,_,_,_))),
val(null), val(null), val(null), val(null), raddr(_,_)).

p(addr(8), ngh, 0, _, pconx(s,o,n,_,_), val(fun(cons,argdes(n,n,_,_))),
ptr(6,ptrconx(_,_,_,_,_)), val(nil), val(null), val(null), raddr(_,_)).

p(addr(9), ngh, 0, _, pconx(s,s,n,s,_), val(fun(ite,argdes(s,n,n,_))),
ptr(10,ptrconx(_,rqd,rqd,_,_)), ptr(14,ptrconx(_,_,rqd,rqd,_)),
val(bool(false)), val(null), raddr(_,_)).

p(addr(10), ngh, 0, _, pconx(s,n,n,o,_),
val(fun(get_structure,argdes(n,n,n,_))), val(int(symb('f/3'))),
argsel(2), argsel(3), val(null), raddr(_,_)).

p(addr(11), ngh, 0, _, pconx(s,n,_,_,_), val(fun(head,argdes(n,_,_,_))),
argsel(2), val(null), val(null), val(null), raddr(_,_)).

p(addr(12), ngh, 0, _, pconx(s,n,_,_,_), val(fun(head,argdes(n,_,_,_))),
ptr(13,ptrconx(_,rqd,_,_,_)), val(null), val(null), val(null),
raddr(_,_)).

p(addr(13), ngh, 0, _, pconx(s,n,_,_,_), val(fun(tail,argdes(n,_,_,_))),
argsel(2), val(null), val(null), val(null), raddr(_,_)).

p(addr(14), ngh, 0, _, pconx(s,s,s,_,_), val(fun(land,argdes(s,s,_,_))),
ptr(15,ptrconx(_,rqd,rqd,_,_)), ptr(24,ptrconx(_,rqd,rqd,_,_)),
val(null), val(null), raddr(_,_)).

p(addr(15), ngh, 0, _, pconx(s,n,n,_,_),
val(fun(assign,argdes(n,n,_,_))), ptr(11,ptrconx(_,rqd,_,_,_)),
ptr(11,ptrconx(_,_,rqd,_,_)), val(null), val(null), raddr(_,_)).
```

```
p(addr(16), ngh, 0, _, pconx(s,n,n,_,_),
val(fun(assign,argdes(n,n,_,_))), ptr(12,ptrconx(_rqd,_,_,_)),
ptr(12,ptrconx(_,_,rqd,_,_)), val(null), val(null), raddr(_,_)).

p(addr(17), ngh, 0, _, pconx(s,n,n,_,_), val(fun(cons,argdes(n,n,_,_))),
ptr(18,ptrconx(_,_,_,_,_)), ptr(20,ptrconx(_,_,_,_,_)), val(null),
val(null), raddr(_,_)).

p(addr(18), ngh, 0, _, pconx(s,n,_,_,_), val(fun(cpp,argdes(n,_,_,_))),
ptr(19,ptrconx(_,_,_,_,_)), val(null), val(null), val(null),
raddr(_,_)).

p(addr(19), ngh, 0, _, pconx(s,_,_,_,_),
val(fun(var,argdes(_,_,_,_))), val(null), val(null),
val(null), val(null), raddr(_,_)).

p(addr(20), ngh, 0, _, pconx(s,n,n,_,_), val(fun(cons,argdes(n,n,_,_))),
ptr(18,ptrconx(_,_,_,_,_)), ptr(21,ptrconx(_,_,_,_,_)), val(null),
val(null), raddr(_,_)).

p(addr(21), ngh, 0, _, pconx(s,n,n,_,_), val(fun(cons,argdes(n,n,_,_))),
ptr(18,ptrconx(_,_,_,_,_)), val(nil), val(null), val(null), raddr(_,_)).

p(addr(22), ngh, 0, _, pconx(s,o,n,_,_), val(fun(cons,argdes(n,n,_,_))),
ptr(6,ptrconx(_,_,_,_,_)), ptr(8,ptrconx(_,_,_,_,_)), val(null),
val(null), val(null), raddr(_,_)).

p(addr(23), ngh, 0, _, pconx(s,n,_,_,_), val(fun(cpp,argdes(n,_,_,_))),
ptr(17,ptrconx(_,_,_,_,_)), val(null), val(null), val(null),
raddr(_,_)).

p(addr(24), ngh, 0, _, pconx(s,s,s,_,_), val(fun(land,argdes(s,s,_,_))),
ptr(16,ptrconx(_,rqd,rqd,_,_)), ptr(25,ptrconx(_,rqd,rqd,_,_)),
val(null), val(null), raddr(_,_)).

p(addr(25), ngh, 0, _, pconx(s,n,n,_,_),
val(fun(assign,argdes(n,n,_,_))), ptr(26,ptrconx(_,rqd,_,_,_)),
```

```
ptr(26,ptrconx(_,_,rqd,_,_)), val(null), val(null), raddr(_,_)).

p(addr(26), ngh, 0, _, pconx(s,n,_,_,_), val(fun(head,argdes(n,_,_,_))),
argsel(2), val(null), val(null), val(null), raddr(_,_)).

p(addr(27), ngh, 0, _, pconx(s,n,_,_,_), val(fun(tail,argdes(n,_,_,_))),
ptr(13,ptrconx(_,rqd,_,_,_)), val(null), val(null), val(null),
raddr(_,_)).
```

The code packets that will create the local variables `U1`, `U2`, and `U3` are those at addresses `17`, `18`, `19`, `20`, `21`, and `23`. The packets at `1` and `2` perform the `data` operation to test if `V` is instantiated. It is necessary to create the output variables `V1`, `V2`, and `V3`; this is achieved by firing the set of packets at addresses `4`, `5`, `6`, `7`, `8`, and `22`. The first argument of the `get_structure` packet, at address `10`, is the functor symbol which the required input compound term has to possess. Its second argument is the input argument that must be decomposed successfully. The third argument is a list of those local variables, `U1`, `U2`, and `U3`, which will hold the arguments of the structure. The parallel tail-fork call of the three `assign` primitives is denoted by the set of packets at `11`, `12`, `13`, `14`, `15`, `16`, `24`, `25`, `26`, and `27`. The use of the `head` and `tail` selector packets is to select the appropriate variables from each list which need to be unified.

Implementing Sequential Search

The sequential search operator: `;`, is modeled using a conditional in the same manner as that used for the sequential conjunction operator: `&`. The representation of the set of clauses `P1 ← G1 : B1 ; P2 ← G2 : B2 .` is shown below.

```
p(_, ngh, 0, _, pconx(s,s,s,n,_), val(fun(ite,argdes(s,n,n,_))),
ptr(_1,ptrconx(_,_,_,_,_)), val(bool(Succeeded)),
ptr(_2,ptrconx(_,_,_,_,_)), val(null), raddr(_,_)).
```

Throttling

It is easy to see that the And-parallelism exploited in this model might lead to the emulated machine being swamped with many short-lived processes. For practical purposes it would be necessary to introduce some mechanism to throttle the parallelism to keep the architecture only as busy as it needs to be to keep all the processing elements active.

Throttling could be quite an expensive mechanism to implement so it is suggested that it should only be done by `and` and `or` constructor packets. This is because it is expected that the bulk of the parallelism is brought about as a result of their execution. The packets would each contain a count of their number of possible active children, which would be in the dormant state waiting to be fired. Each processing element would be assigned a high and low watermark on the number of possible processes it was allowed to possess in a closely-coupled memory system. If the memory model was a physically global shared system there would only be one global set of watermarks provided the global work pool is a single unit.

If the critical number of processes is reached, over the high watermark, the `and` and `or` packets default to "sequential" mode. If there are dormant packets left, the dormant count will indicate this, and they will be fired incrementally until the low active-process watermark is reached at which stage will default back into "parallel" mode. The scheme is simple and is therefore potentially efficient and provides a base upon which to develop a more sophisticated method.

Evaluation

Evaluating the proposed model involved building a simulator, which was written in C. The timings of the various operations and memory access times can be defined at simulation time. There is an array of processor structures which the simulator cycles through simulating active instructions. The number of processors emulated is unlimited to exploit the maximal amount of parallelism available in any program.

A physical implementation of the Packet-Rewriting model would have a target architecture consisting of a number of packet processing agents. Each packet processing agent consists of a processor and memory. This type of architecture is chosen over the physically shared-memory bus design because it appears, on a first examination, to be more scaleable. In order to achieve high-performance it is necessary for the packet agents to be nearing the performance of conventional processors. This is because in order to achieve a significant speed-up of execution, a number of processing elements are required. Timings for instructions (time per cycle), excluding memory references, were based upon a conventional CISC processor, the 68030.

The bit representation used in simulations is shown in appendix 2. Each packet is made up of 386 bits. This is a maximum amount of space needed but it may prove possible to reduce this figure. To model communication timings, the GRIP graph reduction machine [28] [117] [118] memory access time was taken as being similar to that envisaged for the final physical architecture. The timings for GRIP are 400-700 nanoseconds for a local Intelligent Memory Unit (IMU) access and 1000-12000 nanoseconds for a non-local IMU access. The model simulated is independent of any physical memory layout and is based upon a globally addressable packet store. The expected results provide a measure of the maximum possible performance giving an upper bound for what can be expected in a real implementation; overheads are neglected, in particular network contention.

In the Packet-Rewriting model the packets are approximately three times larger than those of GRIP; this assumption is based upon the number of fields in a GRIP packet compared to the number in the model. The maximum possible operating performance of the machine can be benchmarked if all memory accesses are confined to local memory. Due to the larger packet size a memory packet-read or packet-write is assumed to take 3*700 = 2100 nanoseconds.

To evaluate the model two programs are used. These are the `merge/3` program given in chapter 2, which tests the raw performance of a processor and the Takeuchi benchmark, `tak/4`, shown below, which exhibits a large amount of potential parallelism.

```
mode tak(?,?,?,↑).
tak(X, Y, Z, A) ←
    X > Y :
    X1 is X - 1,
    Y1 is Y - 1,
    Z1 is Z - 1,
```

```
    tak(X1, Y, Z, A1),
    tak(Y1, Z, X, A2),
    tak(Z1, X, Y, A3),
    tak(A1, A2, A3, A).
tak(X, Y, Z, Z) ←
    X =< Y :
    true.
```

Consider the `merge/3` program first. The number of packets which would be generated by a compiler for the program is 38. The complete code, analysis and explanation of its runtime behaviour is given in appendix 1. The main results are summarised here. The two input lists are assumed to be of lengths M and N. The table below gives simulation figures for varying values of M and N.

M	N	Logical Inferences	Total Time (mS)	LIPS
25	25	52	13.3	390.2
50	50	102	26.4	388.7
100	100	202	52	387.9

Table 1. *Timings of* `merge/3` *on Packet-Rewriting model.*

M	N	Read Accesses	Write Accesses
25	25	6168	5992
50	50	12168	11842
100	100	24168	23542

Table 2. *Memory Access Behaviour of* `merge/3` *on Packet-Rewriting model.*

The other program used to measure the performance of the Packet-Rewriting model is the Takeuchi benchmark (106 code packets). The `X`, `Y`, and `Z` parameters are varied and the resulting performance measurements are shown below.

X	Y	Z	Logical Inferences	Total Time (mS)	KLIPS
12	3	12	15345	19.4	8
17	12	6	37885	18.3	207
15	6	1	53969	20.6	262
18	12	6	63609	19.4	327
19	12	6	101325	20.6	492
20	12	6	155449	21.7	716
21	12	6	230613	22.9	1009

Table 3. *Timings of* `tak/4` *on Packet-Rewriting model.*

X	Y	Z	Number of Processors	Read Accesses	Write Accesses
12	3	12	1716	3664980	4460709
17	12	6	4004	9100740	11076001
15	6	1	5040	13113816	15958209
18	12	6	6552	15318576	18642897
19	12	6	10192	24456600	29763293
20	12	6	15232	37611336	45771257
21	12	6	22032	55924632	68056101

Table 4. *Memory Access Behaviour of* `tak/4` *on Packet-Rewriting model.*

X	Y	Z	Ratio of LIPS to Number of Processors
12	3	12	4.6
17	12	6	51.7
15	6	1	52.0
18	12	6	49.9
19	12	6	48.3
20	12	6	47.0
21	12	6	45.8

Table 5. *Performance of* `tak/4` *on Packet-Rewriting model.*

The results for the `merge/3` program show a peak performance obtainable of around 400 Logical Inferences Per Second (LIPS). Unfortunately this is approximately three orders of magnitude less performance than that obtainable by today's Prolog hardware implementations for an equivalent Prolog program. For each Parlog process to obtain the same performance for the equivalent Prolog procedure would need at least one hundred times the number of processing elements. The poor performance is due to the copying of code packets and writing them back to store, only for them to be read back later in order to be executed.

If a network bandwidth is assumed that is high enough to allow the transfer of a packet to and from store in the same time, no matter what the width of the packet, the computation time is reduced by three. This would mean a peak performance of around 1.2 KLIPS is obtainable.

The `tak/4` program demonstrates the increase in speed with the size of each computation branch (depth of the search tree) and number of branches (width of the search tree). Normalising the figures by dividing the number of LIPS by the number of processors which are used to provide the performance it is found that each processor is only contributing approximately 50 LIPS.

Summary

Although all of the inherent parallelism of the language Parlog is exploited in the Packet-Rewriting model, this is not without its penalties. The architecture retains a unified code-data policy at the implementation level which models the declarative nature of Parlog. Under simulation, however, the computational model is found to be very inefficient. This is due to the large number of store accesses which are required to rewrite goals into goal systems to be further reduced. A lot of physical work seems to be required to achieve very little when viewed from a language point of view. It has also been found that the fixed size of packet is unsuited to the set of data objects needed in the model. Despite these apparently negative results, the positive effect was that they enabled the development of a new abstract computational model described in the next chapter.

Chapter 5 The Multi-Sequential Coarse-Grain Approach

Multi-Sequential Architectures

In this chapter we describe a new computational model, and the abstract design of a specialised processor, for Parlog. An emulator of a machine called the Parallel Parlog Machine (PPM), consisting of a set of the specialised Parlog processors, is developed to support the Multi-Sequential computational model. The problem with packet-based models is the construction of code packets which are not executed immediately but are written back to memory to be executed later. In the Multi-Sequential model all code is generated at compile-time and stored in an area of memory called the code space. In the Packet-Rewriting model the right-hand side of a clause is stored as a set of code packets which are fetched individually as needed and are transformed until a final result packet is obtained. In the Multi-Sequential model the execution context of the right-hand side of a clause is buffered in a set of registers and the code is written to reference these registers. This eliminates the construction of intermediate code, and result packets, that was a feature in the Packet-Rewriting model and a major source of its inefficiency.

Von-Neumann architectures are very successful because of their close coupling of memory to processor, and very efficient sequence of generated object code. It would seem a sensible approach to try to support a language such as Parlog upon a model which is based upon a duplication of fast sequential Von-Neumann processing elements. If most of the memory references a processor makes are local to the processing element, then, to an outsider looking in, the appearance will be that of a set of autonomous conventional architectures all executing efficiently. The PPM is designed as a loosely-coupled processor-memory pair machine, which improves its potential scaleability compared to that of a conventional shared-memory computer architecture.

Variables will be represented by words in memory. It is possible to bind variables to other variables; this suggests the memory should be organised to provide a global address space to all the processors. Thus the memory management scheme needs to trap non-local references. However in the simple emulation performed here the first few bits of a memory reference are an identifier denoting the processing element to which the reference actually refers. For instance, a memory address is represented diagrammatically as :

Processing Element Identifier	Address On Identified Processing Element

Figure 5. *Memory address representation in the PPM.*

In C , a reference is represented as :

```
struct memory_address {
    unsigned pe_id : 24
        unsigned pe_address : 32
} ;

typedef struct memory_address MEMORY_ADDRESS ;
```

Code Space

The executable code space is separated from the memory area used to store data. This is to ensure better locality of code references to segments/pages of code that will have been referred to previously. In a real physical system or a high-performance abstract machine, the instructions are encoded as a sequence of bytes where one ordercode is stored in a single byte. In the prototype emulator designed here, speed is compromised somewhat to enable the quick development of a working abstract machine. All Parlog object files are sequences of integers. This still allows quick loading and moderately fast instruction decoding. In the description of the abstract machine below the C version of the data structures is given. The actual instruction set supported is given in appendix 3.

Data Space

The user-visible data items that need to be represented inside the model are constants (integers, functors and atoms, and for efficiency, the empty list `nil`), lists, structures and unbound variables. The data space of the emulated architecture consists of an array of value cells. Each value cell is tagged to enable the emulator to tell the difference between different sorts of data at runtime (tags are 8 bits wide, data up to 56 bits). In addition it is possible to atomically "lock" any value cell in the data space.

Integers are represented by tagging the cell with `int`. The rest of the value cell contains a representation of the integer. Floating point numbers are represented by a `fpt` tagged cell. The contents of the value cell reference a further set of cells representing the value of the number. These are not implemented in the emulator but the cells would be a representation of the standard IEEE format for words representing floating point numbers. Functors are represented by a `con` tagged cell. The content is an index into a symbol table or dictionary which contains a representation of the functor. Uninitialised cells are distinguished in the model. This allows a processing element to tell which of its argument registers have never been used. They are tagged with `nul`.

Structures are represented as tuples of cells. A cell is specially tagged with `str` to indicate that the item of data is a structure. The contents reference the tuple of cells making up the actual structure. The referenced cell will be tagged `tpz` for tuple size. Its contents represent how many contiguous value cells follow the `tpz` cell to construct this tuple. The next cell will be a `con` tagged cell representing the functor for this structure. The next group of cells represent the structure's arguments; there is one cell per argument. Lists are a very commonly used data structure and are treated specially in the model. There is no tuple for lists and hence no explicit "`.`" functor cell as such. A list structure is denoted by a `lst` tagged cell. Its contents reference two contiguous cells; the first of which represents the head of the list and the second represents the tail. The empty list `nil/0` is a constant and is represented by a specially tagged cell `nil`.

There are two other data structures employed by the basic model, thus two extra tags are used. The first is `tsk` (task) and is used to denote a special cell used to reference units of work where a unit of work is a branch of the KP-And-Or proof tree; these units of work are represented as tuples. The second tag denotes that the cell contents refer to an instruction in the code space; these cells are tagged as `cod`. These cells are typically found in the units of work tuples where their content is the current code pointer associated with that item of work.

Unbound variable cells are tagged with `unb`. The content of the cell is a reference to itself; this then makes it very easy to bind variables together (described below). A `ref` tagged cell contains an address of another value cell. When binding two unbound variables together, one is chosen to reference the other. This cell is tagged with `ref`. The contents of the `unb` cell are then used to overwrite the `ref` tagged cells contents. The `unb` tag means that there is no need for special hardware to compare the contents of the referencing cell with the contents of the referenced cell and then to test for the end of a reference chain.

A technique called "short-circuiting" is used when dereferencing chains of `ref` tagged cells. If a chain of several `ref` cells is followed, and at the end is a `unb` cell, the head of the chain is overwritten by the `unb` cell's contents so the next time the value of the variable is sought the chain does not have to be searched. The decision is arbitrary as to which `unb` tagged cell to make a reference cell, when binding two variables together, except for the case where one is local and the other non-local. The non-local `unb` tagged cell's contents will be altered so it references the local cell in an attempt to minimize the number of non-local references. Ifa non-variable is found at the end of a chain then the final value cell overwrites the original first reference cell. Only the head of the chain is altered because otherwise, with the chain possibly spanning several memories, there would be a need for locking and altering remote cells which could prove to be expensive.

In C the format of a memory cell is :

```
struct memory_cell {
    unsigned tag : 8 ;
        union {
         MEMORY_ADDRESS memory_reference ;
         int integer_value ;
    }
}
typedef struct memory_cell MEMORY_CELL ;
```

A memory cell is 64 bits wide. The first 8 bits are used to hold the tag and the other 56 bits are available for data. The data field can be either a memory reference, in the case of `fpt`, `ref`, `con`, `tsk`, `str`, `lst`, and `cod`, or an integer for the `int` and `tpz` cases (the last 32 bits contain the integer), or unused, as in the `unb`, `nul`, and `nil` cases.

Diagrammatically the cells are depicted below (the cells are all the same physical size).

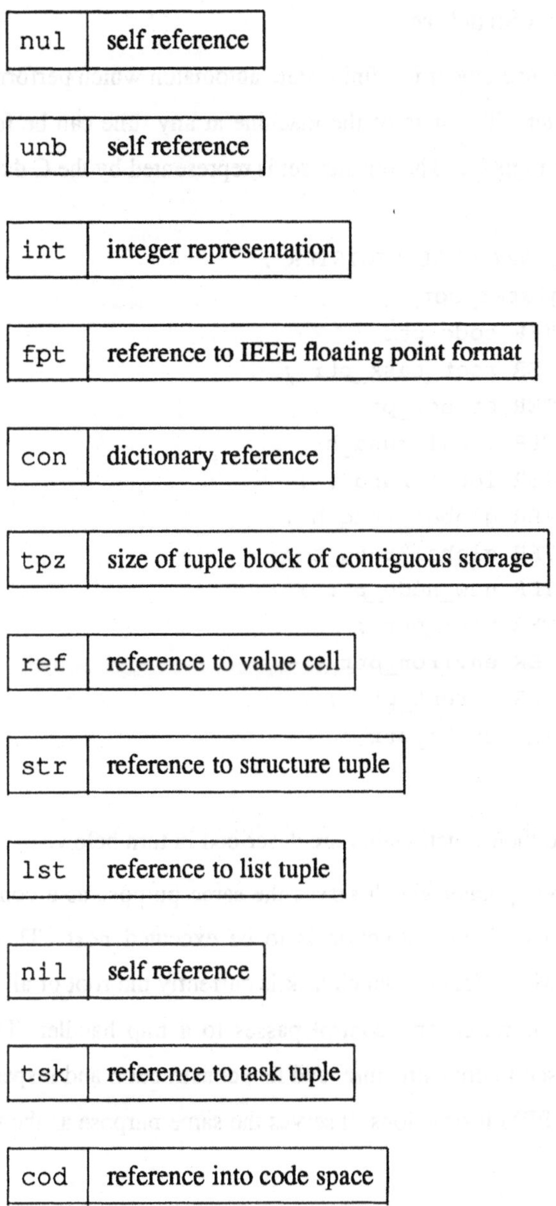

Figure 6. *Representations of data objects in the PPM.*

In the emulator both memory areas are two sub-arrays of a larger array which itself represents physical main memory.

Processing Element Structure

Each processing element is a finite-state automaton which performs operations upon a number of registers. The state of the machine at any time can be found by inspecting the contents of the registers. The register set is represented by the C data structure :

```
typedef MEMORY_CELL REGISTER ;
struct register_set {
     REGISTER code_ptr ;
     REGISTER root_task_ptr ;
     REGISTER struct_ptr ;
     REGISTER local_runq_h ;
     REGISTER local_runq_t ;
     REGISTER global_runq_h ;
     REGISTER global_runq_t ;
     REGISTER new_node_ptr ;
     REGISTER task_ptr ;
     REGISTER environ_ptr ;
     REGISTER parent_ptr ;
     REGISTER child_ptr ;
}
```

These registers and their functionality are described in turn below.

There is a code pointer which serves the same purpose as a conventional program counter and denotes which instruction is to be executed next. There is the root-task identifier register which denotes which task is currently the root of all others. If this fails then an exception is raised and control passes to a trap handler. There is a structure pointer which is used in both structure, and list, construction and inspection. This register is manipulated by PPM instructions, it serves the same purpose as the structure pointer in the WAM.

There are two types of runnable-task identifier queues in each processing element. These are the local and global runnable task queues. On the global queue are placed identifiers of possible runnable tasks which can be executed by any processing element in the system. These are tasks for which a substantial amount of processing should be associated. The local queue is used to hold identifiers of short-lived tasks and built-in operations. To enable manipulation of these queues there are two registers associated with each queue. These are the local runnable head and tail registers and the global runnable head and tail registers. All addition and removal of work takes place through the manipulation of these registers.

In addition there is the "new node" register which holds the identifier of a newly constructed node in the system. This is used to build new subtasks and new control nodes. The identifier of the currently executing task is also held in a register, "task identifier", as it is frequently required in conjunction with the "new node" register. Every task executes in a current environment described below. A reference to this environment is held in the "environment" register. It is frequently used on reloading of awakened and context-switched tasks. There is a reference to the "parent node" in the And-Or execution tree. This is used by tasks when notifying their failure or eventual success. There is also a reference to the descendant node, the "child node" register; this is updated when the task is suspended.

Environments

Every task executes in an environment. For a currently executing task its environment is held in a set of argument registers, labeled "a0", "a1", "a2", ..., etc. Instructions expect to find and manipulate values found in these registers. For tasks which are suspended, or are candidates for execution elsewhere (for instance because the processing element is otherwise occupied) the environment has to be stored in the data area of memory. An "argument vector", or "a-vector", is used. This is simply another data structure associated with the system. The a-vector is stored as a tuple of shadowed argument registers. On rescheduling, the argument registers can be reloaded from the a-vector. In the current version of the emulator 16 argument registers are provided.

If a task is not going to overwrite any of its argument registers then the environment of its parent can be inherited. There is an indicator for the currently executing process denoting if its environment is inherited or is its own. The C data structures are :

```
#define INHERITED 0
#define OWN       1
int environ_type ;
#define NO_OF_ARGS 16
typedef REGISTER[NO_OF_ARGS] a_vector ;
```

Task Data Structures

Suspended and currently unscheduled tasks must be held in memory. The contents of a task structure node is a subset of the machine registers. It is held in the same way as other structures are held in memory, that is, as a tuple. Among the information stored is the code pointer for this process and a reference to its parent node, which can either be a control node or a task node. To distinguish between the two different sorts of parent nodes the reference can be tagged, the parent node can be inspected, or a special indicator stored. In the emulator two different arguments of the structure are used, one for parent task nodes and one for parent control nodes. If its parent is a control node, there is a reference to a control table. As is the case with the parent node references in the emulator there are two sets of arguments to the node structure, one if the child node is a task and another set if the child node is a control node. There is a pair of arguments for each type of child node. One denotes the identifier, a reference to it, and the other is its status. This allows a failed node to kill off any of its descendants. There is also a reference to the environment of this task along with its type.

The current status of the task is also held in an argument of the task data structure. Possible states are `succeeded`, `failed`, `dormant`, `active` and `suspended`. There is a cell which is used as a lock which must be acquired before the task can be updated in any way. There is also a cell which can be used for continuation or choice-point information. That is, if the task succeeds and there is continuation information then it will load its code pointer with the information and proceed as normal. If the task fails and there is choice-point information then the task will load its code pointer with the code address and proceed as normal.

A task which moves into the suspended state must be chained to the variable upon which it is awaiting instantiation. There may be more than one task on this chain so it must be possible to attach the task to another task as well as a variable. On instantiation of variables the task binding the variable must be able to traverse the set of suspended tasks and wake them up. To accomplish this the tasks are chained together as a doubly-linked list. The tasks have a "suspended on reference" argument which either points to the variable or another task which was suspended on the variable earlier. There is also a corresponding "backwards task chain reference". This is used to unblock all the suspended tasks when the variable becomes instantiated. A task must also be able to remove itself from the queue if it is killed or else mark the task in some way so the instantiating task traversing the chain will not attempt to reschedule a dead process. This is discussed in detail below in the section on queue handling and locking.

Control Data Structures

There are two sorts of control nodes, the "Shallow-Or" and the "And". Each of these data structures has an argument describing the type of the node. Since the search tree takes the form of a "Shallow-Or-And-Tree", parents of tasks are usually control nodes. If the situation occurs where a task wishes to inherit the environment of its parent task then there will be two indirections to follow, one of which must pass through the control node. If the task has been distributed out to another processing element then there must be one non-local reference but, because of the extra indirection, there will also be another such reference which could prove expensive. On creating a child control node, before a Shallow-Or- or And-Fork, the environment register is copied into the control node. This allows any child task to inherit its parent environment,even if the parent environment is non-local, by a simple lookup at a given offset from the contents of parent control node field.

In order to tell if a Shallow-Or- or And-Fork has succeeded or failed as a whole, the control nodes must know how many of its child processes are still active or have not been activated yet. As every child task is spawned, the active child task count is incremented. The number of potentially runnable tasks that have not been activated, and as such do not physically exist, is stored in the dormant task count. This allows retroactive parallelism to be employed in the same manner as the PEPSys model of ECRC [6] [19] [20] [75] [180]. In the emulator, however, retroactive parallelism (just enough parallelism is exploited to keep all processing elements busy) is not exploited; that is task data structures are created for every possible child task at the same time. The interaction between task failure and success with the corresponding control nodes is discussed below.

On commitment or failure, children of a control node may have to be killed in certain situations. In order to be able to perform this termination there is a control table associated with each control node but these tables are only created when needed and the reference to the table remains null if unused. The control table itself is just another structure (each item is a value cell). Its representation is depicted below.

tpz 2*N	reference1	status1	...	referenceN	statusN

Figure 7. *Control table representation in the PPM.*

If there are N child tasks then the control table is of size 2*N+1 value cells of contiguous memory and the first of these is a `tpz` cell. As in every structure, its contents are the integer representation of 2*N. For each child task there are two cells. The first is a reference to the task which enables the task to be killed. The second contains the current state of the child and is there primarily to ensure that a task is not submitted to the killing procedure if it no longer exists.

Each control node must be linked into the Shallow-Or-And-Tree, and to do this, there is a link to the parent node in the tree. The parent node could be a control node or a task node so there are two different arguments. If the parent is a control node then there is also a "parent control node table reference". If the task changes state it needs to change its relevant state cell in the parent control table.

The last component is a commitment status flag. These are used only in the Shallow-Or nodes. In the emulator the control nodes are of different sizes but in a physical implementation it could be easier to have both types of control node be the same size, to dedicate a piece of memory to holding control nodes and to manage it with a free-list. The way in which the status flag interacts with failure and success is discussed below.

Tasks can either succeed, fail, remain suspended or reduce perpetually. For each of these states, the tasks will interact differently for each type of parent node. These possibilities are discussed, in turn, below. Only the succeeding and failing states require tasks to interact with their parent nodes.

Consider the case where the task succeeds and its parent is a task node. The parent node will be suspended. The task sets its own status to `succeeded` and then reschedules the parent task. In reality the state corresponding to the newly activated parent task is used to initialise the current processing element, which continues execution with the awakened task. This is an optimisation which is generally used throughout the model where, if an idle processing element activates a task, it continues execution with that task. If a task fails and its parent is a task node, the parent is activated and the processing element initialised with its state, but execution proceeds by jumping to the failure routine to resume backtracking.

A task's interaction with its parent control node is now considered. If a task succeeds and its parent is an And control node then what happens depends upon whether or not it is the only remaining active child. This can be discovered by examining the active child count. Firstly the active count is decremented and if it is not zero then execution continues by calling a "look_for_work" routine. If the count is zero then the success routine is called for the parent control node.

If the current task has failed and the parent is an And control node then the active count is first decremented. If the count is now non-zero then all of the remaining active subtasks must be killed, which is done by inspecting the control-table for the And node and forking off a "kill" process for each active entry. Regardless of the value of the active child count, a specialised control-node failure routine is called.

The other type of parent control node is the Shallow-Or. If the task in question has succeeded then it will attempt to commit. It does this by locking the parent control node and attempting to set the commit flag. If it is not successful then a clause for this procedure has already been "committed to" and the task dies and its table entry is set to succeeded to enable the garbage collection algorithm to perform correctly. On the other hand if it is successful then all of the other remaining active guard computations must be killed. This is done by scanning the control table and, for each active entry, forking off a "kill" routine and setting the status to `failed`. In the current version of the simulator, dead tasks are marked as such and are not removed from any queues they may be on; they are removed as queues are traversed during the course of normal execution. Execution then proceeds by continuing with the instructions making up the body for the clause. In both of the above cases the lock on the task is subsequently released and the active child count is decremented.

The only other remaining case is when a task fails and its parent node is of Shallow-Or type. The active child count is decremented. Its status slot in the control table is set to failed. If its active count is non-zero then the child simply dies. If it is zero then it must be the last child in the disjunction and the specialised control node failure routine is called.

To implement sequences of disjunctions the choice-point field in task data structures is used to store the code address for the start of the next literal of the disjunction. If a task fails and this address is non-null then execution proceeds by loading its code pointer with the address which enables a swift continuation through to the next sequence of clauses. If the information was stored in a control node a costly initialisation of a new task would have to be performed.

Management of Queue Data Structures

In the model's implementation a doubly-linked list of elements (a queue in this context) is a common data structure, in particular for runnable task queues and suspended-on-variable queues. Queue management algorithms are described below which allow concurrent access of the head, tail, and random elements. It must be ensured that locking and access operations are ordered in such a way as to allow safe interleaving and maximum efficiency, in terms of keeping as many tasks active as possible.

It is assumed that it is possible for any processing element to lock any individual value cell. This is necessary to allow consistent updating of data structures in the system. There are two situations in the system where deadlock could occur, even with this mutual-exclusion protection. Deadlock can happen when task destruction interacts with updates of either of the runnable task queues and suspended-on-variables queues. In these cases it is possible for locks to be held on two independent queue elements by two processing elements, but in order for execution to proceed each processing element requires the other lock. The model does not preclude the use of intelligent memory units (IMUs), which perform the locking themselves, instead of it being carried out by the processing elements which makes the implementation simpler.

In the case of the suspended-on-variable queues it has to be possible to allow newly suspended tasks to be added to the tail of the queue, together with the waking up of tasks (because the variable has been bound) by a traversal of the queue from the head, and, concurrently with these, the removal from the queue of any suspended task which has just been killed. In the case of the runnable task queues it must be possible to allow new active tasks to be scheduled by adding to the tail of the queue, together with the scheduling of tasks by removing them from the head of the queue, and concurrently with these actions the removal of now dead tasks from any position in the queue.

A single queue-management algorithm suffices to deal with all of the above mentioned cases. The queue may be in one of three different states when queue interaction happens, and each of these is considered below. The three states are when the queue in question is empty, it contains only one element, or it has two or more members. It is possible to distinguish between these queue states by inspecting the head and tail references for the queue.

Consider the case where a task data structure is being added to a queue. The task structure will itself be locked and in an active state, remaining so until unlocked. If the parent node has decided that the task should be dead, it will have to wait until the whole queue addition operation has finished, before killing the task. This approach is to obviate the need for complicated rollbacks, where the task has to keep a history of everything it has done so far. While performing these rollbacks it would also have to invoke rollbacks for any other task which might also possibly be accessing the queue. In a distributed environment this is expected to be too costly.

If the contents of both the head and tail reference cells are both null then the queue is empty. The tail reference cell is locked, ensuring no other task will see an empty queue and thereby attempt to attach itself (thus possibly causing an inconsistency in the state of head and tail reference cells). The only other form of queue access that could possibly be happening simultaneously on the empty queue is that of the processing elements attempting to remove a task at the head of the queue. Here the processing elements would first inspect the head reference cell. The contents of this will be null and thus the processing elements will give up. Therefore there is no need to lock the head reference cell. The tail reference cell is updated to refer to the task structure and is then unlocked to allow the initiation of another queue addition operation. The head reference cell is then updated to point at this task (an atomic memory write). Note that any other queue addition operation cannot interfere with this one since the task structure is still locked. Finally the task structure is then unlocked.

The case where the queue contains a single element is detected by observing that the contents of the head and tail reference cells are identical and non-null. There will be a reference to the task in the queue from its parent node. Thus the situation may arise where the control node will attempt to kill the task existing in the queue, and ultimately attempt to remove it. A killer process will firstly attempt to lock the task data structure it is attempting to kill. Thus, the task attempting to add itself to the queue firstly locks the head reference cell. It then attempts to lock the task which is already on the queue. If it cannot, it will unlock the head reference cell and go to the start of the queue addition process again, cycling until it eventually adds itself to the queue. Any other task which may be trying to add itself cannot lock the head reference cell and hence will also be forced to cycle around the algorithm. A task which wants to add itself to the queue will eventually lock the task already present. The task to be added can now lock the tail reference cell and make the two tasks refer to each other, thereby chaining in the required task. First the head reference cell is then unlocked, then the original task followed by the added task, and finally the tail reference cell.

The other case to be considered, is when there are two or more tasks already in the queue. This is detected by observing that the head and tail reference cell contents are non-null and different. Notice that if there are more than three tasks, it should be possible to allow the front task to be removed, whilst adding to the back of the queue. To ensure this the locking operations must be done in a prescribed order. Firstly, the locking of the tail reference cell is attempted, then locking the last element of the queue, and finally the last but one element in the queue. If any of the locking attempts fail then all of the locks which have been acquired are released. If they are successful then the task to be added is chained into the queue and the locks acquired are released in reverse order to that in which they were acquired.

There is also one other combination of head and tail reference cell contents that could occur, namely, when they are both different, but one of them is null. In this case it suffices to return to the start of the queue addition algorithm because this situation signifies that an empty queue is part way through having a task added to it, or a single element queue is part way through having its element removed.

To remove a dead task from a queue, the task and its two neighbours have to be locked. If any of these locks cannot be acquired, then all of the locks which have been acquired so far, are released. Because the set of locks that are needed to accomplish each operation is quite small, this approach ensures that execution will eventually proceed. If the memory is organised into intelligent units (having some processing capability) then these locking attempt operations can be issued as one request and serviced atomically.

Load Balancing

Complex load balancing schemes can be very expensive; because of this a simple algorithm is used. Each processing element has a set of nearest-neighbour processing elements. This is a virtual neighbourhood system and need not reflect the physical topology of the architecture. For each element of the set there is a busy/nonbusy indicator. If there is available work on a processing element's global runnable task queue, then each item of work is a candidate to be farmed out to another processing element. A nonbusy processing element is selected at random from the set of workers indicated as being nonbusy. Its indicator is flipped to the busy state and the task is transferred. The only way the indicator can now revert to the nonbusy state is if the specified processing element asks for work.

The other situation to consider is when a processing element is idle. In this case, the processing element will inspect its indicator set looking for busy processors, and then request work from one of them. The chosen busy processing element sets the requesting processing element's indicator, in its processing element set, from busy to nonbusy indicating that the requesting processor is idle. If there is work available, it will be granted and farmed out. The whole conversation consists of busy processors asking idle processors if they want work, if they do not then they are ignored. At the same time idle processing elements are asking busy processing elements if they can have some work; if not then the idle processing elements go to sleep until they are once again asked if they want some work. In a more sophisticated emulation or physical architecture, it would expected to multiplex several virtual workers on one single processing element; which would tend to reduce the amount of time that the processing elements spend idle. In the emulator, indicator sets are implemented as bit-vectors. This requires less communication and knowledge of global state than the case where idle workers search for work.

There is obviously a need for a decision algorithm for putting work on the local or global runnable task queues. In the current version of the emulator, all of a processing element's additional work, is put on its global runnable task queue. One optimisation would be to put work on the global queue only if it represents a call to a user-defined relation but this assumes that system-defined predicates have been optimised into very fast sequential code. The next step would be to use abstract interpretation to identify the complexity of each relation in terms roughly of how many logical inferences are associated with it. Using this, a compiler could annotate each relation and generate code appropriately.

When farming out work, the issue of binding environments has to be considered. An influencing factor on the strategy is that there can be a lot of short-lived tasks. The situation must be avoided where the whole environment of a task is transferred between processing elements, only to see the task quickly fail. As such, environment closing [36], where all arguments of task are fully dereferenced and copied, is rejected as it would be too expensive. The attitude taken here, is to attempt to transfer as much information across processing elements, in order to allow tasks to decide whether they should fail, depending on the type of their arguments. In the majority of cases, clauses seem to be written so that their left hand sides are nonoverlapping, and there is a genuine non-deterministic choice to made between those clauses that do have overlapping consequents.

Only enough of each argument is transferred to identify its principal functor. Each `ref` tagged cell is fully dereferenced and short-circuited before being transferred, in order to avoid chasing down chains of non-local references. All other tagged cells are transferred as they stand. As a result, the environment management scheme is lazy, and values are only obtained when wanted. Two other possible additions to the information to be transferred are the principal functors of the subterms of a structure and the principal functor of the first element of a list.

In every argument vector many of the value cells may be unused and because of this, it is unnecessary to transfer the whole vector. The unit of information transferred is a minimalist argument vector simply called a "minimal a-vector". In the emulator there is a maximum of sixteen argument registers. A bit-vector is used to denote which registers are in use. The integer representation of this bit-vector is constructed as an integer value cell and precedes any a-vector elements which are transferred. The integer value cell allows the receiver to reconstruct the original a-vector.

Thus, if only the first four shadowed argument registers are in use, then the bit-vector is `0000000000001111` and the corresponding integer is `15`. The minimal a-vector is shown below.

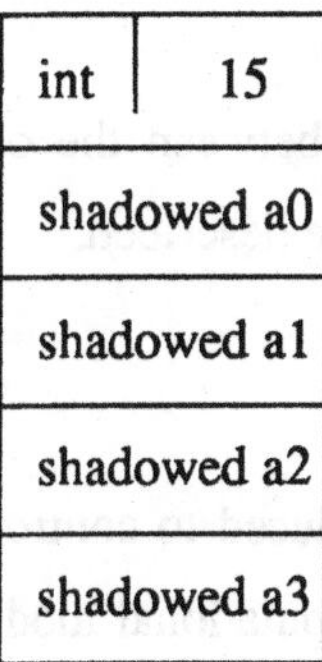

Figure 8. *Example of a transmitted a-vector in the PPM.*

Recovery from Resource Exhaustion

An execution model for Parlog must exploit And-parallelism. Tasks suspend when encountering an unbound variable which they expect to be bound. In practice there is a limit to the number of tasks present at any time. Thus it is possible to obtain a situation whereby an architecture can be full of suspended processes and there is not enough memory available to start other tasks which might produce a binding to awaken any of the suspended tasks. If this situation is reached the execution can never complete. However, if the search tree had been explored in a different manner the execution would never have blocked.

A solution proposed here is to destroy one of the suspended processes thus freeing memory. This is relatively expensive but cheaper than performing no computation at all. Destroying a process will involve interaction with both a suspended variable list, and a suspended task list. A task would then be chosen for extermination, its parent control node located, and the task's status reset to the unstarted (dormant) state. A dormant process has now to be chosen to be scheduled, in the hope that it will relieve the deadlock situation and bind some variable upon which a task is suspended. A search is made from the destroyed task, upwards in the tree, for a dormant task, whose control node has an a-vector which contains a reference to the variable which the (now killed) task was suspended on. The task located in this way may be a sibling task or a task associated with an ancestor but in either case this task is now activated.

Abstract Instruction Set

In this section the differences between the original SPM instruction set and the newly-devised PPM instruction set are described.

Shallow-Or Control Instructions

Two new instructions are introduced to control Shallow-Or parallelism that occurs in the KP-And-Or-Tree abstract computational model. There are two different situations that have to be controlled; these are the cases where the relation consists of more than one Shallow-Or fork and the other, a specialisation of the first, where a relation consists of a single Shallow-Or fork. These relations, `H1` and `H2` respectively, are shown below :

```
H1 ← G1  : B1 \\
 .       .
 .       .
H1 ← Ga  : Ba ;
H1 ← Ga+1  : Ba+1 \\
 .       .
 .       .
H1 ← Gb  : Bb ;
H1 ← Gb+1  : Bb+1 \\
 .       .
 .       .
H1 ← Gn  : Bn .

H2 ← G1  : B1 \\
H2 ← G2  : B2 \\
 .       .
 .       .
H2 ← Gn  : Bn .
```

The second case is the simpler and thus is dealt with first. The new instruction is

```
try_committed_or_fork([label(_1), ..., label(_n)]).
```

The argument of `try_committed_or_fork/1` consists of a list of labels. Each label refers to the code for each individual clause of the Shallow-Or fork. The semantics of the instructions are :

(i) suspend current task.

(ii) create a Shallow-Or fork control frame.

(iii) make environment pointer in new control frame equal to that of the environment pointer in the suspended control frame.

(iv) nullify choice point field in the new control frame as this is only a single Shallow-Or fork.

(v) double-link the suspended and new control frames together.

(vi) create control table and link to control frame.

(vii) spawn tasks and update control table as needed.

(viii) choose one of newly spawned tasks for further execution.

The first case is slightly more complicated because if the first set of clauses fails to provide a candidate the next set must be tried. The instruction introduced is :

```
try_committed_or_fork_else([label(_1), ..., label(_n)], label(_else)).
```

The first argument of `try_committed_or_fork_else/2` is again a list of labels, one for each of the clauses in the Shallow-Or fork. The second argument is again a label, only this time it refers to the code to be executed should any of the forked clauses fail to produce a candidate clause. The semantics of the instructions are :

(i) suspend current task.

(ii) create a Shallow-Or fork control frame.

(iii) make environment pointer in new control frame equal to that of the environment pointer in the suspended control frame.

(iv) set choice point field in the new control frame to `label(_else)`, this indicating the next set of clauses to try should all the guards of the forked tasks fail.

(v) double-link the suspended and new control frames together.

(vi) create control table and link to control frame.

(vii) spawn tasks and update control table as needed.

(viii) choose one of newly spawned tasks for further execution.

And- Control Instructions

There is only one And-Control instruction. This is

```
spawn_and_fork([label(_1), ..., label(_n)]).
```

The argument is a list of labels each referring to a code sequence for each of the conjuncts in the parallel And- fork. The semantics of the instruction are :

(i) suspend current task.

(ii) create an And fork control frame.

(iii) make environment pointer in new control frame equal to that of the environment pointer in the suspended control frame.

(iv) double-link the suspended and new control frames together.

(v) create control table and link to control frame.

(vi) spawn task and update control table as needed.

(vii) choose one of newly spawned tasks for further execution.

Code Generation Examples

The code generated for all of the different types of Parlog relation is given here.

Sequential Or

```
H ← G1 : B1 ; % H has arity M
H ← G2 : B2 ;
H ← G3 : B3.
```

```
label(h).
environ_own.
allocate(M, 0).
try_committed_or_fork_else(label(c1)).
G1.
commit_own.
B1.
label(c1).
environ_own.
allocate(M, 0).
try_committed_or_fork_else(label(c2)).
G2.
commit_own.
B2.
label(c2).
G3.
B3.
```

In the above `label(h)` is the code entry point for this predicate. The `environ_own` instruction sets the environment flag in the child task structure so when it is executing it knows that it has not inherited its parent's environment. The `allocate(M, 0)` instruction copies the environment of the parent process, `M` argument registers, for the child ensuring that a guard does not overwrite the environment should it not succeed. The last clause does not need to use this two-instruction combination because if the code for it is executed then there are no other clauses left, thus if it fails the predicate will fail. The `try_committed_or_fork_else/1` instructions are used for trying the clauses sequentially. The `commit_own` instruction performs the required commitment operation once it is known that the task executing the instruction is a candidate.

Parallel Or

```
H ← G1 : B1 \\
H ← G2 : B2 .

label(h).
allocate(M, 0).
try_committed_or_fork([label(c1), label(c2)]).
par_proceed.
label(c1).
environ(own).
allocate(M, 0).
G1.
commit_own.
B1.
label(c2).
environ(own).
allocate(M, 0).
G2.
commit_own.
B2.
```

In this case both clauses need their own environment, since they run in parallel and either guard can potentially modify its environment. The `try_committed_or_fork/1` instruction performs the necessary book-keeping to set up the potential for parallel execution of the two clauses.

Sequential/Parallel Or

```
H ← G1 : B1 \\
H ← G2 : B2 ;
H ← G3 : B3 .
```

```
label(h).
try_committed_or_fork_else([label(c1), label(c2)], label(c3)).
par_proceed.
label(c1).
environ(own).
allocate(M, 0).
G1.
commit_own.
B1.
label(c2).
environ(own).
allocate(M, 0).
G2.
commit_own.
B2.
label(c3).
G3.
B3.
```

Here the `try_committed_or_fork_else/1` is used to set up a control frame in which two child tasks can be started for the first two clauses and the choice point field is set to reference the code for the third clause should both of the first two fail.

Parallel/Sequential Or

```
( H ← G1 : B1 ;
  H ← G2 : B2 ) \\
```

```
H ← G3 : B3 .

label(h).
try_committed_or_fork([label(c1), label(c2)]).
par_proceed.
label(c1).
try_committed_or_fork_else(label(c11), label(c12)).
par_proceed.
label(c11).
environ(own).
allocate(M, 0).
G1.
commit_own.
commit_own.
B1.
label(c12).
environ(own),
allocate(M, 0).
G2.
commit_own.
commit_own.
B2.
label(c2).
environ(own).
allocate(M, 0).
G3.
commit_own.
B3.
```

In this, the most complex form of Parlog relation, a parallel-fork must be set up in which the first item is itself a sequence of clauses to be tried in order. Thus a `try_committed_or_fork/1` is used to set up the control structure enabling the architecture to execute this fork. The `par_proceed` instruction is used to return control back to the caller after execution has succeeded. The first label of the fork will reference code to execute the first sequence of clauses (this is the reason for the presence of the `try_committed_or_fork_else/2` instruction). Therefore there will be two Shallow-Or control structures between either of the first two task structures and the parent, so two `commit_own` instructions are required for each clause to ensure commitment.

Sequential And

```
H ← D & E .

label(h).
% put arguments for call to d
spawn_and_fork(label(dpre)).
% put arguments for call to e
execute(e).
label(dpre).
execute(d).
par_proceed.
```

This is the code for a single clause. Its environment and control (within the procedure) is assumed to be already generated. There is a sequence of `put` instructions generated first to set up the arguments in their correct registers for the clause. The `spawn_and_fork/1` instruction sets up a control frame allowing the first clause to be executed and suspending the parent task. If the first conjunct is successful the parent will wake up and then execute the `execute/1` instruction jumping to the code for the final conjunct.

Sequential/Parallel And

```
H ← (D, E) & F.

label(h).
spawn_and_fork([label(dpre), label(epre)]).
```

```
% put args for call to f
execute(f).
label(dpre).
% put args for call to d
execute(d).
par_proceed.
label(epre).
% put args for call to e
execute(e).
par_proceed.
```

In this clause a parallel conjunct is executed and only when it is successful is the last conjunct executed. Thus a `spawn_and_fork/1`, with arguments being the labels of the conjuncts to be executed in parallel, is first executed. Then, when this is successful, the `execute` instruction is executed to jump to the code for the final clause.

Simulation of Model

The complete PPM has been simulated in two different stages. The first simulator is an architecture simulator written in C. The output of this stage is a detailed trace of all events that occur during execution. The emulation trace becomes the input for the final stage of the PPM simulation. This stage is written in Prolog and simulates any parallelism that may be present at any time in the program.

A single processor version of the PPM abstract machine was developed because of the lack of a real parallel machine upon which to experiment. This also allowed the instruction set to be verified much more quickly than in the case of a real implementation, due to there being only a single local runnable task queue and no shared data structures between processing elements. The simulation of the parallelism was done using a Prolog program because of the expected short development time using a declarative language.

Static Emulator

The PPM Static Emulator resembles both the WAM and SPM in that it behaves as a bytecode interpreter. It emulates the PPM at the abstract instruction level. It consists of a main dispatch loop which branches, using the order code of the instruction it is currently executing, to the correct C routine to emulate that instruction. The machine uses two separate areas of memory : "code space" and "data space". The data space is itself split into two parts : "symbol table/dictionary" and "value cell space". In the Emulator these are implemented as three separate arrays of structures; each of the spaces having a separate structure for their elements. Locking is simulated in the Emulator but only as a memory-write operation (in this simple implementation, a lock operation consists of setting a lock associated with the word). Special care is taken over a distinguished task in the system called the "root process". If this process fails then the machine fails as a whole; it is tantamount to an operating system failure. In the present version of the Static Emulator task-killing is not implemented. If a process And-forks then the leftmost process is cached for execution locally on the forking processor.

The result of a simulation is a trace file recording various events that take place during execution. These include : the dereferencing of a value cell; dereferencing of a register; the cacheing of a task; an instruction failure; commitment attempts; the allocation of new value cells; and the beginning and end of an instruction-execution cycle. Other information which is needed for the next stage of the simulation is also collected. This includes : the type of instruction being executed; the value of all the machine registers at the beginning and end of each execution cycle; and the current runnable task queues at these times.

From a trace file it is possible for the dynamic simulator to extract information to allow it to simulate a machine exploiting all the parallelism that is available. The order that the search tree is expanded is, however, breadth-first but the leftmost branch is always chosen. This is one possible behaviour of a real PPM and thus the results can be considered to be valid.

Dynamic Simulator

The dynamic simulator is written in Prolog [17] [18]. It simulates the PPM at a more abstract level than the architecture emulator. Unlike the emulator, however, it does simulate parallelism. The user is allowed to set the number of processors for each simulation of an emulator trace file.

The simulator accumulates various information for each processor. This includes : a unique identifier; a clock; the current task it is executing; its current global and local runnable task queues; a list of non-local references; and the current instruction it is executing. The use of each one of these is explained below in the detailed operational description of the simulator.

The first action the emulator takes is to read the trace file and to transform the event listing into a sequence of instructions. This sequence of instructions is then further transformed into a set of PPM tasks. The initial task is marked as such.

At the start of each fetch-execute loop for an instruction, a processing element is selected. This is the one which is to be chosen for execution on this cycle of the simulator. The processing element which is chosen is the one with the lowest clock value that has work available. The simulator then "executes" this instruction. This includes calculating the times to fetch the instruction from memory; accessing, and if necessary dereferencing, the relevant argument registers; and any time taken for writing values into the data space. Also included are the times taken to manipulate any control structures (such as on task commitment, failure or success). The times used as estimates for memory access are those taken from the hardware GRIP emulator [28] [117] [118]. This machine consists of several closely-coupled processing-element/memory-element boards connected via a bus. Thus is it quite similar to the envisaged PPM physical architecture, a loosely-couple processor-memory pair architecture. The time for a local-board memory access is 0.4 to 0.7 nanoseconds per word, and for a non-local-board access it is estimated to be 1.0 to 1.2 microseconds. The reading time for literal type argument registers is counted as being negligible.

The time taken for the execution of this instruction is then added to the clock of the processing element which executed it and the clocks of any other processing elements which are idle at that time.

Any other active tasks which are created by the execution of the instruction are then scheduled for execution on any of the idle processing elements. As part of the emulation trace file, the current state of the runnable task queues is given at each instruction execution cycle. However, these states relate to the PPM Static emulator, which is sequential, being only used for detailed emulation and verification of the abstract instruction set. In the parallel simulator, some of the tasks in the runnable task queue at a particular time in the trace, may have already been farmed out and scheduled on other processors. Thus, before distributing a task to another processing element in the trace's runnable task queue, a check is performed to see if it is indeed present in the task set (compiled as the first part of the simulator's activity). If it is not then the next task in the runnable task queue is processed, unless this is empty. If it is a real active task, it is added to the runnable task queue of a selected idle processing element and removed from the simulator's global task set. The time for this task farming-out operation must be calculated. It is assumed that the transfer of information does not coincide with, and thus hold up, any other possible concurrent information transfers. The task structure for this active task (15 value cells) plus its argument vector (17 value cells) needs to be transferred. This amounts to 31 value cells of information. This is because the two `tpz` cells from these two structures can be stripped off and the result is packaged into a new structure of 30 value cells, requiring a new `tpz` cell. The time is calculated as 31 non-local data space reads. Also included in the farm-out time is the time taken to load up the argument registers of the receiving processing element from the argument vector. This amount to reading 16 values cells from local data space memory. Many processors may farm out many tasks. The farm-out time is taken for the processor farming out the largest number of tasks. This farm-out time is then added to the clocks of all the architecture's idle processors.

As part of the information kept for each processing element, there is a set of non-local references. The reference to the task to be distributed out to another processing element and the reference to its argument vector need to be made non-local on the processor performing the farming out of work. This is most simply done by adding these references to its non-local references set. Then when any of these references is dereferenced, the access can be trapped by looking in this "non-locals" set and the time for a non-local dereference recorded. The destination processor may also have to update its set of non-local references. If any of the task's argument registers are valid references, then these are now non-local and should be added to the destination processor's set. Also to be added are any parent control-node and any parent control-table references.

After calculating the task distribution time and updating any idle processors the simulator will iterate again choosing another processor for execution of an instruction-fetch-execute-loop. This will continue until the simulator's global task queue is empty and all of the processors are idle.

One defect of the current simulator arises because it simulates the activity of the sequential emulator. As result, the order of commitment of tasks is exactly the same as in the emulator. For a Shallow-Or-fork, the task that eventually commits, if there is one, is the one that committed in the emulator run. This behaviour is acceptable, however, because in a truly parallel machine the times for commitment and farming out of Shallow-Or-siblings are unpredictable and can only be found by real implementation on a real machine. Indeed the simulation represents one of the many possible ways in which the search space can be traversed, and it does not violate any Parlog operational semantics.

At the end of the simulator run a set of statistics is produced. These include : the final state of each processing element; how many tasks have been executed; how many instructions have been executed; and the number of data space value cells allocated.

It was discovered during the development of the PPM simulator that Kish Shen had written a simulator for the Argonne model of Or-parallel Prolog [144]. It is also written in Prolog and is quite similar to the PPM simulator. It is interesting to note that a complete simulation run in Shen's model also consists of two stages. There is a static stage and a dynamic stage.

During the static stage a program is executed by a basically sequential Prolog engine. This phase generates as output the search-tree with only Or-parallel nodes retained. It is called a shape-tree because enough information is stored in the Or-nodes for the dynamic stage of the simulation to reconstruct the shape of the search-tree. This is similar to the PPM emulator, in that a sequential engine is used, but in the PPM case more information is recorded.

As in the PPM simulator, Shen's dynamic simulator recreates parallelism. It differs in that the simulator switches between tasks only at task completion. The PPM simulator switches between tasks after the completion of each instruction. This provides a more realistic model of parallelism than Shen's simulator as it simulates tasks running concurrently.

Results

It is possible to run any size program upon the Static Emulator but there were time constraint problems associated with using the output from the Static Emulator as the input to the Dynamic Simulator. Running the Dynamic Simulator with large traces was not practical because the SICStus Prolog engine could not run the simulation in a reasonable time. It should be noted that this is not a problem with SICStus Prolog but with the technology used to implement Prolog : C or assembler emulator loop on a sequential processor. The space requirements for a trace of the execution of a program with a large search tree were great. For these reasons it was decided to study several small programs which create lots of small processes with large communication overheads, in an attempt to investigate the worst possible performance figures for the simulated architecture.

The first chosen program was a quicksort of six integers in reverse order, as shown below :

```
mode sort(?, ↑).
sort(List, Sorted) ← qsort(List, Sorted, []).

mode qsort(?, ↑, ?).
qsort([U|X], Sortedh, Sortedt) ←
 partition(U, X, X1, X2),
 qsort(X1, Sortedh, [U|Sorted]),
 qsort(X2, Sorted, Sortedt).
qsort([], Sorted, Sorted).

← sort([6, 5, 4, 3, 2, 1], Sorted).
```

The corresponding PPM assembly code generated and executed is given in appendix 4.

The total number of basic machine instructions executed was 795, the number of value cells consumed was 3802 and the number of tasks created was 110. A task was created to solve each literal of the Kernel Parlog version of quicksort. The table and graphs below illustrate the performance of the PPM executing the quicksort program.

Number Of Processors	1	2	4	8	12	16
Microseconds	7965	4289	2539	1717	1604	1630
KLIPS	13.8	25.6	43.3	64	68.6	67.5
Speedup	1	1.8	3.1	4.6	5	4.9

Table 6. *Timings for quicksort on the Multi-Sequential Model.*

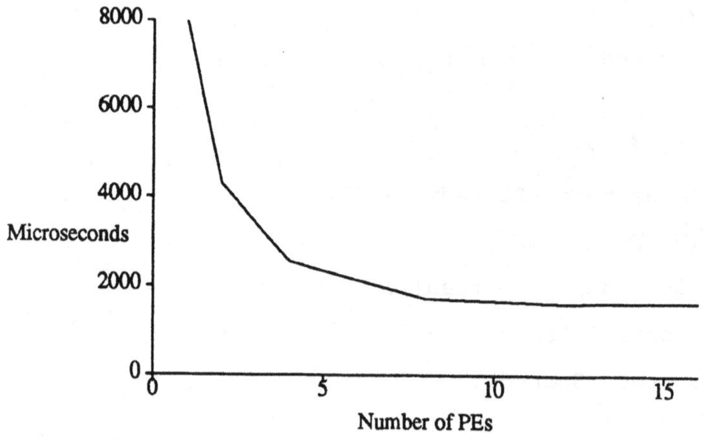

Graph 1. *Execution Time vs. No. of PEs for quicksort on the Multi-Sequential Model.*

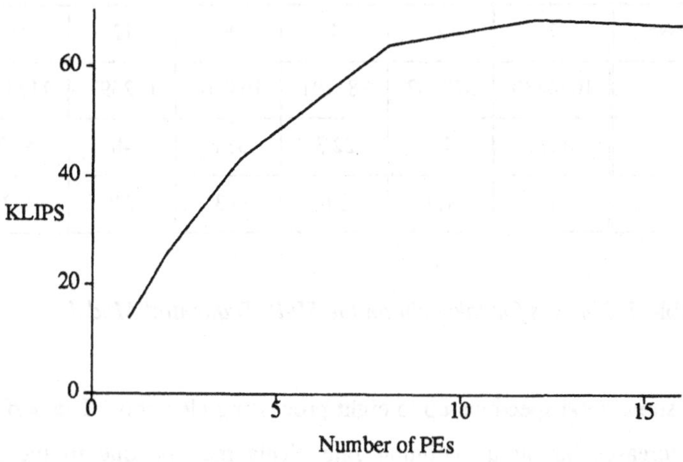

Graph 2. *Speed vs. No. of PEs for quicksort on the Multi-Sequential Model.*

On this particular program, the architecture scales reasonably well up to 8 processing elements then very little is gained in performance by adding more processors. In fact performance tends to peak and then degrade suggesting that this particular program should be run on a configuration not exceeding 8 processing elements. It is hypothesized that the performance degradation, if more than 8 processors are used, is probably due to the average number of active processes over time being 8, and that of the limited amount of parallelism present in the quicksort algorithm. Even so the speeds obtained are of the order of two magnitudes better than that of the fine-grain model.

The takeuchi benchmark, given in chapter 4, was also used. The call was `tak(18,12,6,X)`. The results are summarised in the table below.

Number Of Processors	1	2	4	8	12	16
Microseconds	1024830	528262	284791	163916	132597	117360
KLIPS	6.2	12	22.3	38.8	48	54.2
Speedup	1	1.9	3.6	6.3	7.7	8.7

Table 7. *Timings for takeuchi on the Multi-Sequential Model.*

The results show good speedups up to eight processing elements. The performance from then on increases but at a declining rate. This may be due to the dynamic simulator's imposed ordering upon the search strategy used. The performance figures are summarised in the following two graphs.

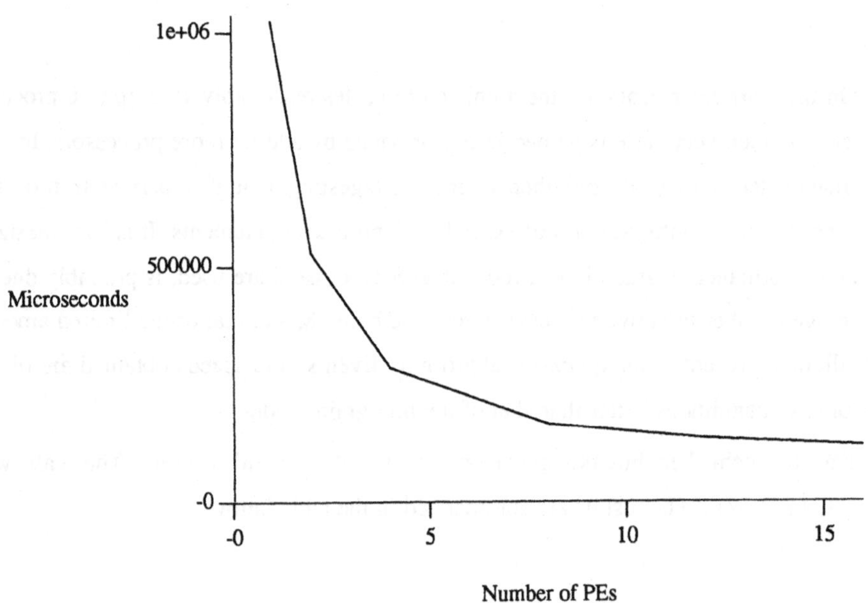

Graph 3. *Execution Time vs. No. of PEs for takeuchi on the Multi-Sequential Model.*

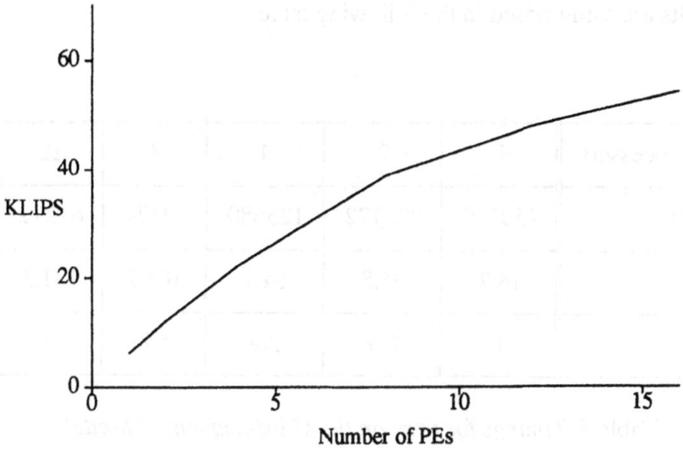

Graph 4. *Speed vs. No. of PEs for takeuchi on the Multi-Sequential Model.*

The last example program was naive reverse of a list of thirty integers. The program is shown below :

```
mode nrev(?, ↑).
nrev([U| X], Z) ← nrev(X, Y), append(Y, [U], Z).
nrev([], []).

mode append(?, ?, ↑).
append([U| X], Y, [U| Z]) ← append(X, Y, Z).
append([], X, X).
```

The results are summarised in the following table :

Number Of Processors	1	2	4	8	12	16
Microseconds	430110	225172	125680	74174	61272	56506
KLIPS	18.7	35.8	64.1	108.7	131.5	142.6
Speedup	1	1.9	3.4	5.8	7	7.6

Table 8. *Timings for nrev on the Multi-Sequential Model.*

These results are also summarised in the following two graphs.

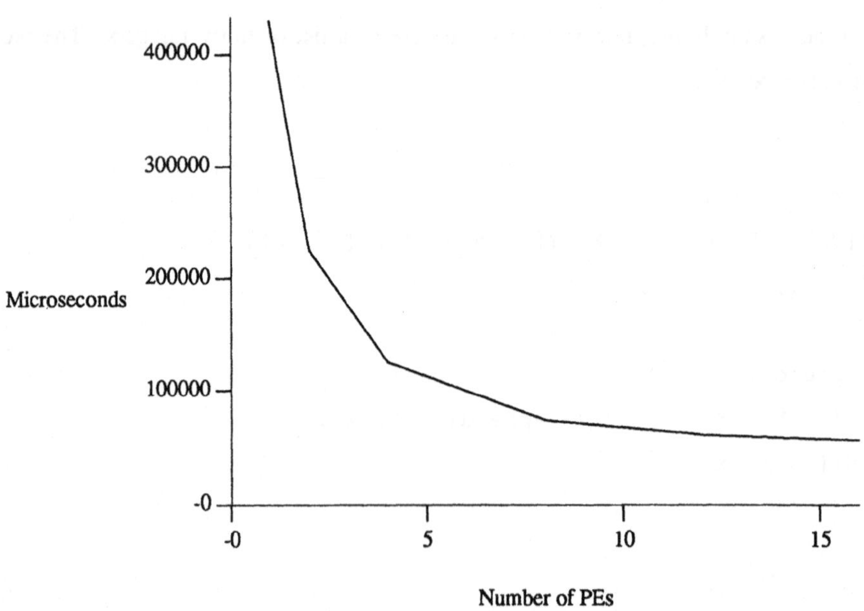

Graph 5. *Execution Time vs. No. of PEs for nrev on the Multi-Sequential Model.*

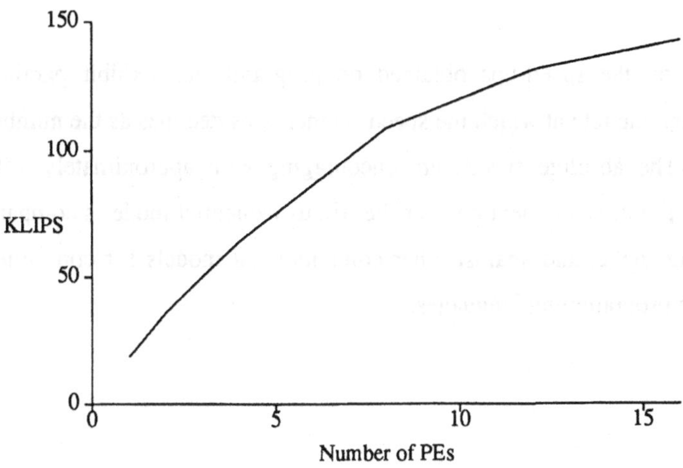

Graph 6. *Speed vs. No. of PEs for nrev on the Multi-Sequential Model.*

The speed-ups for naive reverse increase but the rate at which this happens decreases as the number of processors becomes larger. This is a common factor with all the experiments that were run. The overall speed was encouraging; it was possible to achieve 150 KLIPS with 16 processors. The memory access time for a GRIP processor board turns out to be approximately 10 to 20 times longer than that of a conventional machine such as a Sun3. If the normal memory had been used instead of the Intelligent Memory Units (IMUs) present in the GRIP architecture then it may be hypothesised that the performance would be much greater. A lot of the functionality of memory management such as garbage collection is moved into the IMUs in the Grip architecture so it is difficult to compare the two different processor-memory architectures. The processor used in a GRIP processor board is a conventional 68000 thus the processor speed is comparable to that of many other conventional computer systems.

Summary

In conclusion the speed-ups obtained on programs that exhibit parallelism are promising, though the rate at which the speed-up increases declines as the number of processors grows. The absolute speeds are encouraging with approximately 150 KLIPS achieved at one point. In the next chapter the Multi-Sequential mode is compared to the Packet-Rewriting model and against other computational models for committed-choice concurrent logic programming languages.

Chapter 6 Summary, Further Work and Conclusions

Introduction

In this chapter both the Packet-Rewriting model and the Multi-Sequential model are compared against other similar computational models that have been developed. The two computational models, developed during the course of this research, are then contrasted with each other and the differences analysed. This is followed by a discussion of possible future work which could follow on from the research. Finally the results are summarised and conclusions from them are drawn.

The Packet-Rewriting Model

The Alice graph-reduction machine [41] [42] has a similar computational model to that of the fine-grain Packet-Rewriting model discussed in chapter 3. Unlike the Packet-Rewriting model, Alice makes explicit the difference between code and data at the physical implementation level. Data is represented as packets which are very similar to the Packet-Rewriting model's code/data packets. Code is treated very differently however. All equations making up a program are transformed into a language called Alice CTL (Compiler Target Language) [126] [127] [128] which will, when executed, construct data packets representing the code. This is different to the Packet-Rewriting model where the data packets for the code are constructed at compile-time and merely need to be loaded into memory, along with the code packets, to form the executable program. Thus the Packet-Rewriting model is more efficient since Alice must create these code packets at runtime.

The And-Tree model of Parlog computation is currently being implemented upon Alice. Flat Parlog forms the basis of the transformation of Parlog into KP-And-Tree [96]. The Parlog data structure representation used in the Alice And-Tree model is almost identical to that of the Packet-Rewriting model. A Parlog variable is represented by an Alice variable packet [43]. A Parlog constant is represented as an Alice constructor packet. The Alice machine allows packets to suspend upon the event of a referenced packet becoming a constructor or a variable packet. Parlog calls are represented by Alice rewritable packets. There is one Alice CTL rewrite rule for each Flat Parlog procedure. In the Packet-Rewriting model each rule is represented by a separate set of packets. This is less expensive than in Alice where the code for the complete predicate is fetched.

The process of finding and selecting a candidate clause is an atomic action performed in one evaluation step by an Alice processing element. In contrast, only commitment need be atomic in the Packet-Rewriting model. Any explicit parallelism involved with this search is simulated within the processing element; in the Packet-Rewriting model any parallelism can be exploited. While performing the search the processing element will construct a set of variables which are required to be instantiated in order for reduction to succeed and then will use this information to suspend the call packet if it is non-empty. Whereas in the Packet-Rewriting model a matching goal is activated when its input argument is instantiated, in the Alice model there is one unification process which is only activated when all of the input arguments are sufficiently instantiated for the head of a clause to match with the calling goal. This is because Alice provides a mechanism whereby packets can suspend, waiting for a set of argument packets to be rewritten to constructor packets. Thus in the Packet-Rewriting model suspended clause tasks are woken up sooner than is the case with Alice. The only packets that are created by the use of a CTL rule are the body packets corresponding a selected candidate clause. Alice CTL is an intermediate language enabling the easy implementation of functional languages. It does, however, require modification from its present form before it can be used to efficiently implement Parlog.

The first approach to implementing Parlog on Alice was in fact based upon the KP-And-Or-Tree model. One of the drawbacks of this version was that all of the packets of the bodies of all clauses for a relation were constructed regardless of whether they were candidates or not. In the Packet-Rewriting model this has been avoided because of the incremental nature of the packet-copying i.e. the only body packets copied are those for the body of the candidate clause committed to.

It is interesting to contrast the approach taken here, of compiling Parlog directly into the Packet-Rewriting Model CTL, with the approach currently proposed by the Alvey Flagship group. In their declarative system world an intermediate language is used called DACTL (Declarative Alvey Compiler Target Language) [68] [69] [70], although at present only a syntactic subset of this is used which is called MONSTR (Maximum of One Non-root STateholder per Rewrite) [4]. All programming languages supported by Flagship are first compiled into MONSTR which is then compiled into Flagship machine code.

Both Imperial College (IC) and the University of East Anglia (UEA) are currently working on implementing Parlog on top of MONSTR. In the IC approach [96] Parlog is firstly compiled into "Very Flat Parlog". Very Flat Parlog is just a limit case of Flat Parlog where the guard contains only matching primitives. The implementation of Parlog uses the And-Tree model of execution discussed in chapter 1. The Very-Flat Parlog program is then transformed into sets of DACTL rules. For each Very-Flat Parlog procedure there are three types of DACTL rules generated. These are rules corresponding to the procedure's suspension, success, and failure. There is one success rule for every Very-Flat Parlog clause, and normally only one rule for suspension and one for failure. The DACTL rules are themselves ordered; all the success rules must be tried, followed by the suspension rule, which both must be tried before the failure rule. There are a substantial number of DACTL rules for each Very-Flat Parlog procedure because deep matching of arguments is compiled out. This will effect the level of granularity of computation greatly. The effect of this increased computation per Parlog procedure upon the execution speed of the Flagship architecture has not yet been assessed. Compared to the code used by the Packet-Rewriting model there are at least three times as many rewrite rules, the amount of work performed is substantially more, and each item of work being much more fine-grain.

In the UEA approach [67] [115] Parlog is translated into an intermediate form of Kernel Parlog called "KP_{DACTL}". This a variant of Kernel Parlog in which repeated variables are not allowed in input arguments; new variables are introduced for any repeated occurrences and calls to the test unification primitive, to test equality of the repeated variables, are added to the guard of a clause. All output arguments are distinct variables. If any of these do not have explicit assignment goals associated with them, for them to output match, then calls to a full unification primitive are introduced. All guards and bodies containing sequential conjunction operators are transformed into new conjunctions in which parallel conjunction is the only operator used. This will introduce unnecessary parallelism and synchronisation (the UEA model uses shared variables for synchronisation to simulate the sequentiality) compared to the Packet-Rewriting model which does support sequential conjunction operators. The restriction on the input arguments is because DACTL's pattern matching mechanism can be used directly for matching invoked by KP_{DACTL} clauses. There is no need to add a unification primitive for an output argument that does its output matching by use of an explicit assignment primitive because DACTL directly supports the overwriting of variables.

Unlike the IC model, the UEA scheme, as in the case of the Packet-Rewriting model, is centred around Parlog's And-Or-Tree model of computation. An earlier attempt to support Parlog via DACTL [113] [114] was based upon the And-Tree computational model. However DACTL's full potential for parallelism was not realised because a single process was introduced to simulate any Or-Parallelism in a program. DACTL was first translated into KP-And-Tree which, on reflection, is inherently inefficient compared to DACTL. DACTL is a more flexible language than Parlog because it is meant to be a CTL rather than a programming language; it thus enables efficient code to be generated more easily. Flattening a Parlog clause causes some original guard goals to appear in the body of the target Flat Parlog clause. This goal location information is therefore not available to the Flat Parlog → DACTL compiler leading it to generate inefficient code in some cases.

A possible improvement over the Packet-Rewriting model would be to adapt it to the current Flagship Architecture [72] [137] [178] [179]. The computational model is different to the one described in [177], in that equations are not compiled into sets of template packets but into sequences of serial code (Idealised Instruction Set Code, IIS) which is stored in variable length code packets (CODE). It might prove possible to translate Kernel Parlog directly into IIS. Although using packets would be an overhead compared to the coarse-grain approach taken in the PPM, the resulting implementation would be faster than the current fine-grain one. This approach could be regarded as a fine-grain PPM model where code and data are stored in a single heap.

The Multi-Sequential Model

In this section other Multi-Sequential Parlog models are discussed and contrasted with the PPM. Many of the other models reported in the literature have no associated results so the places where they differ from the PPM are pointed out and possible differences in performance examined.

The model proposed by Crammond in [37] is, as is the case for the PPM, a variation of the KP-And-Or-Tree computational model. The architecture consists of a set of processing elements, each having its own local memory, each connected to a shared global memory. The global memory is divided up into 3 parts : static part to hold the compiled code, dynamic part containing environment bindings, and the process part containing information for each created process. In the model there is a special processor dedicated to running a scheduler which allocates work to the processors. Unlike the PPM this architecture is based around a shared global store model for bindings and as such is unlikely to scale-up and perform efficiently. The scheduler could prove to be a source of inefficiency since the processing elements themselves do not do their own scheduling and thus may not be able to take advantage of locality of data properties. In the PPM scheduling is local to each processing element and this allows scheduling decisions to be made independently. In the model described in [37] the scheduler is very centralised and may be a bottleneck as the number of processing elements grows.

In [38] a model is devised to support general committed-choice non-deterministic concurrent logic languages (Concurrent Prolog, Parlog and GHC). Thus the instruction set of the machine is much more general than that of the PPM. In this model the mechanisms to enable process killing are not present; processes will execute until they fail or succeed. In the PPM these mechanisms are present and this needless computation avoided. The environment binding management scheme is not discussed in any detail but indications are that it is again based upon a local and global frame system as is [37].

In Crammond's thesis [40] an abstract machine is described which is a combination of the And-Or- and And-tree models. It was developed at the same time as the research reported here. Since then however the model has been refined and is more And-Tree biased [39]. Both of these engines have been implemented upon real parallel hardware.

Experiments using Crammond's first model were performed upon a 20 processor Sequent Balance. For naive reverse the best speed-up was 12, on quicksort it was 7, for the takeuchi benchmark it was 15, and a version of the layered queens program performed with a speed-up of 15. The absolute speed for nrev was 30KLIPS on 20 processors; the processor on the Balance is approximately 3.5 times slower than that of the performance of the Sun 3/75 processor.

The programs that were used to benchmark the PPM were quicksort, takeuchi and naive reverse. The absolute speeds using a single Balance processor for these programs on Crammond's first model were 1.25 KLIPS, 0.9 KLIPS, and 2.6 KLIPS respectively. For the PPM, the single processor speeds are 13.8 KLIPS, 6.2 KLIPS, and 18.7 KLIPS.

Using these figures it can be seen that a PPM processor is of the order of a 10 times faster than that of a Balance processor emulating Crammond's abstract machine.

However, apart from single processor performance, it is impossible to directly compare Crammond's implementation on the shared-memory Sequent Balance against the loosely-coupled processor-memory pair PPM. Memory access time for the Balance is constant, ignoring bus contention, whilst for the PPM there is a local memory access time and a non-local memory access time. Crammond's timings are from a C implementation of an abstract machine whilst the PPM is a dedicated hardware architecture.

Performance figures for a newer model, based on KP-And-Tree [39], are all for naive reverse and reported here for completeness. Architectural details of this model have not been reported in the current literature. On the Sequent Balance the speed on a single processor is 3.5KLIPS and on 20 processors is 40KLIPS and for the Sequent Symmetry using one processor the absolute speed is 10.5KLIPS and on 9 processors it is 70KLIPS (on the SPM system on a Sun 3/75 the speed is 14KLIPS).

In [163] a model known as Kelpie is developed which executes And-Parallel Kernel Parlog (APKP) [161]. It is possible to transform both GHC and Parlog into APKP. The methods for this are given in [161]. The model is a task-oriented one much like the PPM. The approach is not a compiled abstract machine one however; APKP source is directly emulated in Kelpie. The implementation of the model is written in C and is targeted to single processor workstations. There is no mention of results, or whether the model is implemented are given, and so it is difficult to compare Kelpie with the PPM. However, as Kelpie is a very-high level emulator, it is unlikely to perform as efficiently as the PPM machine.

Comparison of the Packet-Rewriting and Multi-Sequential Models

There is no distinction between code and data at the implementation level in the Packet-Rewriting model; every data packet created at run-time can, in principle, be executed. This has to be the case since it is necessary for graphs to be created dynamically at run-time and then become candidates for evaluation. In normal logic programming terminology the model is structure copying for both the code and data spaces because for every item of code to be executed or structure to be created, packets must be allocated. The simulation results show that very high raw performance figures are possible but at the cost of using a large number of processing elements. The raw performance of a processor was very poor due to the high number of memory accesses, associated with a logical inference, when performing a rewrite. Code packets are constantly copied and then written to store but then have to be read back to be executed. Thus rewriting a goal to its set of subgoals, the right hand side of the clause with whose head the goal unifies, is very costly.

It appears that the problem with packet-based models is the construction of code packets which are not executed immediately but are written back to memory to be executed later. In the Multi-Sequential model all code is generated at compile-time and stored in an area of memory called the code space. The PPM uses code in a structure-sharing manner and data by structure-copying. For each logical inference a copy of the code is not created; this is a major improvement over the Packet-Rewriting model. In the Packet-Rewriting model the right-hand side of a clause is stored as a set of code packets which are fetched individually as needed and are transformed until a final result packet is obtained. The size of the code and data objects for the PPM are much smaller than that of the Packet-Rewriting model; suspended, ghost flags, and return addresses are not needed for each object. A packet is a constant size in the Packet-Rewriting model whereas in the Multi-Sequential model only the necessary words of memory are allocated to represent data. In the Multi-Sequential model the execution context of the right-hand side of a clause is buffered in a set of registers and the code is written to reference these registers. This eliminates the construction of intermediate code and result packets that was present in the Packet-Rewriting model and a major source of inefficiency.

The Multi-Sequential model can thus be seen as a natural progression from the Packet-Rewriting model as they are very similar if the improvements mentioned above are made. The tasks are not as fine-grain as in the Packet-Rewriting model which, it is hypothesised, is the reason why the raw performance of the Multi-Sequential model is not as good. However the Multi-Sequential model is much more cost-effective in that each processor is capable of executing many more logical inferences per second than processors of the Packet-Rewriting model.

Further Work

Load Balancing and Complexity Analysis

There is a whole field that needs exploring, in the areas of load balancing and scheduling, which is related to that of complexity analysis and compile-time transformation techniques. It may prove possible to obtain a relative number of inferences associated with each relation, compared to all other relations, which would give the system some "weight" information which could be used at runtime. This weight information could also be used at compile-time to fold predicates together to give more coarse-grained predicates (those with a higher weight). This would help performance enormously because the PPM has a very crude load balancing and scheduling algorithm at present : system built-ins must be executed locally and all other tasks are candidates for local or remote execution.

Investigating Massively Parallel Architectures

Massively parallel architectures are now becoming commercially available. It may turn out that a natural computational model for Parlog, and other similar languages, could arise from research currently being pursued on implementing declarative languages on these architectures [111] [7] [158] and so the main features of these machines are outlined below.

In [111] a massively parallel applicative programming system architecture called Apsa is described. It uses SIMD parallelism to support data structures for applicative, functional and logic programming languages. Some algorithms for Apsa, such as the functional aggregate update system, implement data structure operations that are very inefficient on conventional architectures (including MIMD machines). Other algorithms use parallel data structures to directly implement the language reduction model. An example is a parallel stream recursion equation system, which can rapidly evaluate functional programs that have been transformed into a static set of equations in iterative form. This algorithm can also be used as a highly parallel digital circuit simulator. The most important problem in developing such algorithms is to avoid communication bottlenecks that would inhibit parallelism. Apsa uses a binary tree interconnection network, and it relies on hierarchical locality in the data structures to avoid bottlenecks in the tree. The tree network has low latency, and it can execute many key algorithms without excessive message conflicts in the network. An emulation of Apsa on the NASA Massively Parallel Processor is currently operational, and a Connection Machine implementation should also be feasible. A VLSI prototype of a restricted version of Apsa has also been completed. No performance figures are given and so it is impossible to tell if an implementation of Parlog would give impressive performance results; though a drastically different computational model to that of the Multi-Sequential and Packet-Rewriting models would probably be required.

Work reported in [7] centres around the implementation of a language called Uplog on the Connection Machine. The language Uplog is very similar to that of Parlog and FGHC. The abstract machine is known as the Condition Graph Inference Machine and the inference procedure is known as Condition Graph proof; both are described in [7] but no performance figures are quoted. However during the course of the research a "thought-provoking" experiment was carried out on the Connection Machine [158]. A hand-compiled version of naive-reverse was run with a list of 524,288 elements as input. The result was obtained in just over one second. To give an idea of how fast this result actually is, BIM Prolog takes approximately 7 days to compute the result. In fact a Prolog system would need to perform the computation at a speed of 134 GigaLIPS to arrive at the answer in the time taken by the Connection Machine. Thus there appears to be a great potential for executing Parlog at speeds never before achieved.

Making Use of Associative Memory Techniques

Associative memory techniques and hardware unification units may be able to help improve performance marginally; certainly it may help to improve the speed of each individual processing element. Some of the work which may prove helpful in making the individual PPM processing elements faster is now reviewed.

In [131] a hardware unit called the Pattern Addressable Memory (PAM) is presented. Its function is to match strings of symbols, thus improving clause indexing. It does not perform full unification, however, since it does not do unification of variables. However, since full unification is a primitive of the PPM machine, PAM could act as a very fast clause indexing unit since it could perform the one-way input matching efficiently.

A unification processor has been developed at Keio University and is described in detail in [145]. The unification processor seeks to exploit any available unification parallelism. The processor itself is based around the systolic array concept. It also performs the occur check efficiently although this is not a requirement for its use with the PPM. When variables are unified together their values are not shared but copied to every occurrence of the variable. Thus this method does not share structures and some work is required to reduce the size of final unified term.

Work has been done at Syracuse architecture [112] [150] based around using content-addressable memory (CAM) for the rapid execution of Prolog. The hardware is composed of three functional units. The Binding Agent handles the binding of variables to terms, looking up a variable's binding, and retracting a group of bindings. The Heap Processor stores terms in the database and assists in unification of different terms. Finally the Clause Filter reduces possible matching clauses for a given goal. Hardware unification is performed by considering the program and goals as binary trees. The Prolog interpreter was instrumented to obtain an estimated performance figure for a possible INMOS Transputer implementation. Using CAM resulted in a five-fold speed-up for the naive reverse program. The hardware may improve the performance of the PPM similarly, particularly in the area of indexing.

Research carried out at Honeywell Systems and Research Center, Minneapolis has resulted in the development of a Hierarchical Associative Memory Architecture for Unification [141]. Parallelism is exploited at the level of clause selection and unification. Unfortunately a static compile-time analysis is needed to partition frequently-used rules to fast content-addressable memory and lesser-used rules to conventional memory, in the normal manner. Thus the approach for large programs does not appear to be very fruitful for the PPM unless compiler technology is improved substantially.

Memory Organisation

The issue of memory organisation has not been considered in any detail for either computational models. Cacheing [8] [71] has been mentioned as a possible way of improving architecture performance. The interaction between cacheing and logic programming architecture has been explored by the Prolog group at the University of Berkeley [106]. The memory is partitioned into high-bandwidth (HB) memory and synchronization memory. The synchronization memory is used to store synchronization and status information. The synchronization information consists of event flags, lock variables and semaphore variables. The status information includes the status of resources such as processors and buffers, various control flags such as modify, reference and valid cache indicators, and mail boxes. The bulk of an application's code and data, and operating system are stores in HB memory.

The explicit parameter-passing mechanism of logic programs (unification) necessarily means that any supporting architecture performs a large number of memory writes. The published results from Berkeley suggest that having invalidation caches for the HB memory will substantially improve architecture performance at very little cost. Using this scheme the only information that is broadcast by a cache, to its fellow caches, is the fact that it has altered some block in its own local memory. Other caches recognise this fact and will only read in a fresh up-to-date copy of this invalidated block when it is demanded. Because Parlog is a committed-choice programming language, no backtracking is required, there will be fewer memory writes than in the case of the Berkeley Parallel Prolog Processor (PPP) [57] [58], simulated in [106]. Thus this scheme is ideal for exploitation in PPM.

Interfacing to Databases

Work has been done on investigating the way in which Parlog can be used in conjunction with a database of Horn clauses [160] [162]. The approach taken was to write an all-solutions server in C and couple it to Kelpie (discussed earlier in the section on the Multi-Sequential Model). The Kelpie All-Solutions Server (KASS) is accessed through the `set/3` and `subset/3` primitives. Kelpie and KASS share both global heap and symbol table memory space to facilitate the incremental binding of the result variable to a solutions list and the sharing of Horn clause predicate name symbols.

The semantics of `set/3` and `subset/3` as given in [73] are changed slightly. This is because the implementation in [73] relies on a metainterpretation approach with the metainterpreter for the Horn clauses being written in Parlog itself [31]. This approach is too slow and inefficient for serious use thus a new approach was needed. The semantic changes are that

(i) No order-of-satisfaction restriction is imposed upon the solution list for `subset/3`.

(ii) Cuts are not allowed among the Horn clauses in the database.

(iii) The database of Horn clauses contains only all-solutions relations.

KASS is reported to be under construction in [160] and [162]. The intention being to interface the complete Kelpie and KASS systems to a hardware clause retrieval system. Thus the resulting system should enable a multi-user deductive database management system to be written in Parlog using the all-solutions server as a shared inference engine over a deductive database of Horn clauses. It should be possible to directly couple the PPM and KASS giving the PPM a deductive database capability.

Conclusions

Two computational models have been developed for the parallel execution of the concurrent logic programming language Parlog during the course of this research. Parlog at the language level is a formalism for expressing solutions to problems in a process-oriented manner. The first model that was developed, the Packet-Rewriting model, attempted to capture this property at the implementation level in that every object that was created could be considered as a process in its own right (a process context being the fields of the packet). The result was a very fine-grained model that seemed to offer good possibilities of exploiting the available parallelism in Parlog programs. However, when simulated, the Packet-Rewriting model did not perform well in terms of its cost effectiveness. This was because of the size of the work associated with each item of data i.e the "size" of an instruction was very small. The raw performance of the model was very good, thus it has attractions for those programmers who are interested in running their programs as fast as possible, regardless of how many processors are used.

The results obtained from simulating the Packet-Rewriting model led to the development of a coarse-grain model, which was more cost effective. This Multi-Sequential model is based on the notion of using a set of WAM-like processing engines to compute a solution to a Parlog program, thus making use of current logic programming language implementation techniques. The speed-ups obtained were quite promising, although the benchmark programs were rather artificial.

The language Parlog is a very high-level language in which to write concurrent communicating programs. All communication channels are modelled as lists and in fact implemented as lists. Better performance would be achieved if direct inter-process communication were used. This would eliminate the need to build list data constructors around each item of data needing to be transmitted.

The granularity of the parallelism affects the speed-ups one can obtain; the finer the granularity of the implementation, the more available work is required at any time to get good performance. In the Packet-Rewriting model it is hard to get good availability of large pieces of work, due to the very nature of the model, which partly explains why the results were poor. The Multi-Sequential model performed better because a smaller number of items of work were required to get good speed-ups. This tends to suggest that Packet-Rewriting models are not a viable proposition for implementing Parlog due to amount of processor-memory communication involved.

There is a whole issue of a declarative programming style versus an imperative programming style which affects the performance of any language implementation. The lack of destructive assignment certainly affects the programmer's abilities to write efficient programs in some cases. This is especially true in those circumstances where the programmer might want to use an array but, because of the declarative nature of the programming language, uses lists, although a good declarative programmer would use a more efficient data structuring scheme. If the programmer wants to change an element of a data structure in a declarative language, this notionally means making a complete copy of the data structure with a new element in place of the old one which is very inefficient in most cases. However if compilation methods improved it may be possible to overcome this problem by detecting where data structures cannot be shared at runtime, thus allowing the use of destructive assignment.

The Parlog language itself must be reviewed in the light of its effect on performance. The language tends to lead to the writing of inefficient programs. Programs written with parallelism in mind tend to produce fine-grain parallelism. This then tends to encourage the programmer to write programs consisting of coarse-grain parts through the use of sequentialising constructs in both the cases of Shallow-Or and And- parallelism to obtain better performance. This is orthogonal to the usage of Parlog as an architecture-independent parallel programming language. Further research on compilation techniques is needed to improve this situation.

This research has shown that it is possible to construct computational models upon which Parlog program can be executed. Very high raw performance can be obtained using a fine-grained approach although at the expense of using a very large number of processors. It has also shown that a more cost-effective coarse-grain model produces good speed-ups and has better raw performance per processor although the scaleability of such a system has still to be proved and is a topic for further research.

Appendix 1 Fine-Grain Execution of merge/3

The program below is taken from chapter 2 and is used to merge two lists into one.

```
mode merge(?,?,↑).
merge([U|X],Y,[U|Z]) ← merge(X,Y,Z).
merge(X,[U|Y],[U|Z]) ← merge(X,Y,Z).
merge([],Y,Y).
merge(X,[],X).
```

The generated set of code packets is

```
% top-level root packet
p(addr(1), ngh, 0, _, pconx(s,s,n,s,_), val(fun(or,argdes(s,n,s,_))),
val(int(4)), ptr(2,ptrconx(_,rqd,rqd,rqd,_)), val(bool(false)),
val(null), raddr(_,_)).

% 1st Clause
% merge([U|X], Y, [U|Z]) ← merge(X, Y, Z).
p(addr(2), ngh, 0, _, pconx(s,s,o,_,n),
val(fun(clause,argdes(s,n,n,n))), ptr(6,ptrconx(_,rqd,_,_,_)),
ptr(18,ptrconx(_,_,_,_,_)), ptr(24,ptrconx(_,_,rqd,rqd,_)),
ptr(3,ptrconx(_,rqd,rqd,rqd,_)), raddr(_,_)).

% 2nd Clause
% merge(X, [U|Y], [U|Z]) ← merge(X, Y, Z).
p(addr(3), ngh, 0, _, pconx(s,s,o,_,n),
val(fun(clause,argdes(s,n,n,n))), ptr(9,ptrconx(_,_,rqd,_,_)),
ptr(18,ptrconx(_,_,_,_,_)), ptr(24,ptrconx(_,rqd,_,rqd,_)),
ptr(4,ptrconx(_,rqd,rqd,rqd,_)), raddr(_,_)).
```

```
% 3rd Clause
% merge([], Y, Y).
p(addr(4), ngh, 0, _, pconx(s,s,o,_,n),
val(fun(clause,argdes(s,n,n,n))), ptr(12,ptrconx(_,rqd,_,_,_)),
val(null), ptr(35,ptrconx(_,_,rqd,rqd,_)),
ptr(5,ptrconx(_,rqd,rqd,rqd,_)), raddr(_,_)).

% 4th Clause
% merge(X, [], X).
p(addr(5), ngh, 0, _, pconx(s,s,o,_,n),
val(fun(clause,argdes(s,n,n,n))), ptr(15,ptrconx(_,_,rqd,_,_)),
val(null), ptr(35,ptrconx(_,rqd,_,rqd,_)), val(nil), raddr(_,_)).

% 1st Clause - Guard Conjunction
p(addr(6), ngh, 0, _, pconx(s,s,n,s,_),
val(fun(ite,argdes(s,n,n,_))), ptr(7,ptrconx(_,rqd,_,_,_)),
ptr(8,ptrconx(_,rqd,rqd,_,_)), val(fun(fail,argdes(_,_,_,_))),
val(null), raddr(_,_)).

p(addr(7), ngh, 0, _, pconx(s,n,_,_,_),
val(fun(data,argdes(n,_,_,_))), argsel(2), val(null), val(null),
val(null), raddr(_,_)).

p(addr(8), ngh, 0, _, pconx(s,n,o,o,_),
val(fun(get_list,argdes(n,n,n,_))), argsel(2),
ptr(36,ptrconx(_,_,rqd,_,_)), ptr(37,ptrconx(_,_,rqd,_,_)),
val(null), raddr(_,_)).

% 2nd Clause - Guard Conjunction
p(addr(9), ngh, 0, _, pconx(s,s,n,s,_),
val(fun(ite,argdes(s,n,n,_))), ptr(10,ptrconx(_,rqd,_,_,_)),
ptr(11,ptrconx(_,rqd,rqd,_,_)), val(fun(fail,argdes(_,_,_,_))),
val(null), raddr(_,_)).
```

```
p(addr(10), ngh, 0, _, pconx(s,n,_,_,_),
val(fun(data,argdes(n,_,_,_))), argsel(2), val(null),
val(null), val(null), raddr(_,_)).

p(addr(11), ngh, 0, _, pconx(s,n,o,o,_),
val(fun(get_list,argdes(n,n,n,_))), argsel(2),
ptr(36,ptrconx(_,_,rqd,_,_)), ptr(37,ptrconx(_,_,rqd,_,_)),
val(null), raddr(_,_)).

% 3rd Clause - Guard Conjunction
p(addr(12), ngh, 0, _, pconx(s,s,n,s,_),
val(fun(ite,argdes(s,n,n,_))), ptr(13,ptrconx(_,rqd,_,_,_)),
ptr(14,ptrconx(_,rqd,_,_,_)), val(fun(fail,argdes(_,_,_,_))),
val(null), raddr(_,_)).

p(addr(13), ngh, 0, _, pconx(s,n,_,_,_),
val(fun(data,argdes(n,_,_,_))), argsel(2), val(null),
val(null), val(null), raddr(_,_)).

p(addr(14), ngh, 0, _, pconx(s,n,o,o,_),
val(fun(get_nil,argdes(n,_,_,_))), argsel(2), val(null),
val(null), val(null), raddr(_,_)).

% 4th Clause - Guard Conjunction
p(addr(15), ngh, 0, _, pconx(s,s,n,s,_),
val(fun(ite,argdes(s,n,n,_))), ptr(16,ptrconx(_,rqd,_,_,_)),
ptr(17,ptrconx(_,rqd,_,_,_)), val(fun(fail,argdes(_,_,_,_))),
val(null), raddr(_,_)).

p(addr(16), ngh, 0, _, pconx(s,n,_,_,_),
val(fun(data,argdes(n,_,_,_))), argsel(2), val(null),
val(null), val(null), raddr(_,_)).

p(addr(17), ngh, 0, _, pconx(s,n,o,o,_),
val(fun(get_nil,argdes(n,_,_,_))), argsel(2), val(null),
```

```
val(null), val(null), raddr(_,_)).

% set of packets to construct a two element binding list
p(addr(18), ngh, 0, _, pconx(s,o,n,_,_),
val(fun(cons,argdes(n,n,_,_))), ptr(19,ptrconx(_,_,_,_)),
ptr(20,ptrconx(_,_,_,_)), val(null), val(null), raddr(_,_)).

p(addr(19), ngh, 0, _, pconx(s,n,_,_,_),
val(fun(cpp,argdes(n,_,_,_))), ptr(21,ptrconx(_,_,_,_)),
val(null), val(null), val(null), raddr(_,_)).

p(addr(20), ngh, 0, _, pconx(s,o,n,_,_),
val(fun(cons,argdes(n,n,_,_))), ptr(22,ptrconx(_,_,_,_)),
val(nil), val(null), val(null), raddr(_,_)).

p(addr(21), ngh, 0, _, pconx(s,_,_,_,_),
val(fun(var,argdes(_,_,_,_))), val(null), val(null),
val(null), val(null), raddr(_,_)).

p(addr(22), ngh, 0, _, pconx(s,n,_,_,_),
val(fun(cpp,argdes(s,n,_,_))), ptr(23,ptrconx(_,_,_,_)),
val(null), val(null), val(null), raddr(_,_)).

p(addr(23), ngh, 0, _, pconx(s,_,_,_,_),
val(fun(var,argdes(_,_,_,_))), val(null), val(null),
val(null), val(null), raddr(_,_)).


% 1st and 2nd clause - body conjunction
p(addr(24), ngh, 0, _, pconx(s,n,n,_,_),
ptr(25, ptrconx(_,_,_,_)), argsel(2), val(null),
argsel(3), val(null), raddr(_,_)).

p(addr(25), ngh, 0, _, pconx(s,n,n,n,o),
ptr(26,ptrconx(_,_,_,_)), argsel(2), argsel(3),
argsel(4), ptr(18,ptrconx(_,_,_,_)), raddr(_,_)).
```

```
p(addr(26), ngh, 0, _, pconx(s,s,n,s,_),
val(fun(and,argdes(s,n,s,_))), val(int(3)),
ptr(27,ptrconx(_,rqd,rqd,rqd,rqd)), val(bool(_)), val(null),
raddr(_,_)).

p(addr(27), ngh, 0, _, pconx(s,s,_,n,_),
val(fun(clause,argdes(s,n,n,n))), val(bool(true)),
val(null), ptr(28,ptrconx(_,_,rqd,_,rqd)),
ptr(31,ptrconx(_,rqd,rqd,rqd,rqd)), raddr(_,_)).

p(addr(28), ngh, 0, _, pconx(s,n,n,n,_),
val(fun(put_list,argdes(n,n,n,_))), ptr(29,pconx(_,_,rqd,_,_)),
ptr(29,pconx(_,rqd,_,_,_)), ptr(30,pconx(_,_,rqd,_,_)),
val(null), val(null), raddr(_,_)).

p(addr(29), ngh, 0, _, pconx(s,n,_,_,_), ptr(36,ptrconx(_,_,_,_,_)),
argsel(2), val(null), val(null), val(null), raddr(_,_)).

p(addr(30), ngh, 0, _, pconx(s,n,_,_,_), ptr(37,ptrconx(_,_,_,_,_)),
argsel(2), val(null), val(null), val(null), raddr(_,_)).

p(addr(31), ngh, 0, _, pconx(s,s,_,n,_),
val(fun(clause,argdes(s,n,n,n))), val(bool(true)), val(null),
ptr(32,ptrconx(_,_,_,rqd,rqd)),
ptr(33,ptrconx(_,rqd,rqd,_,rqd,_)), raddr(_,_)).

p(addr(32), ngh, 0, _, pconx(s,n,n,_,_),
val(fun(assign,argdes(n,n,_,_))), argsel(2),
ptr(29,ptrconx(_,_,rqd,_,_)), val(null), val(null), val(null),
raddr(_,_)).

p(addr(33), ngh, 0, _, pconx(s,s,_,n,_),
val(fun(clause,argdes(s,n,n,n))), val(bool(true)),
val(null), ptr(34,ptrconx(_,_,_,rqd,rqd)), val(nil), raddr(_,_)).

p(addr(34), ngh, 0, _, pconx(s,n,n,n,_),
ptr(1,ptrconx(_,_,_,_,_)), ptr(37,ptrconx(_,_,rqd,_,_)),
```

```
argsel(2), ptr(37,ptrconx(_,_,_,rqd,_)), val(null),
val(null), raddr(_,_)).

% body for clauses 3 and 4
p(addr(35), ngh, 0, _, pconx(s,n,n,_,_),
val(fun(assign,argdes(n,n,_,_))), argsel(2), argsel(3),
val(null), val(null), val(null), raddr(_,_)).

% routine to get first element out of a two element binding list
p(addr(36), ngh, 0, _, val(fun(head,argdes(n,_,_,_))),
argsel(2), val(null), val(null), val(null), raddr(_,_)).

% routine to get second element out of a two element binding list
p(addr(37), ngh, 0, _, val(fun(head,argdes(n,_,_,_))),
ptr(38,ptrconx(_,rqd,_,_,_)), val(null), val(null),
val(null), raddr(_,_)).

p(addr(38), ngh, 0, _, val(fun(tail,argdes(n,_,_,_))),
argsel(2), val(null), val(null), val(null), raddr(_,_)).
```

In total there are 38 packets. The `or` packet at address `1` is used to link the four `clause` packets together. The clauses are each rooted at `2`, `3`, `4`, and `5`. Each pointer to a `clause` packet has a packet-context which will enable the referenced packet to execute in the context of the call, i.e. have access to the three calling arguments. Each of the first two clauses need to create two new variables, one to hold the head of the input list being matched, the other to hold the new output variable for the recursive call. The packets rooted at `18` will create a two element binding list for this purpose.

The collection of packets rooted at `6` represents the guard for the first clause. The guard requires access to the first argument of the call and the pointer context handles this by indicating it needs the second field of the calling packet. The guard is a sequential conjunction therefore the root is a `&` packet. The second field of the `&` packet is a reference to a `data` packet at address `10`. If this succeeds then the computation will proceed with the `get_list` packet at address `11`, indicated by the third field of the `&` packet.

The data packet requires the second field of the calling packet, the parent clause packet, to proceed. The pointer context for the pointer field referencing 10 indicates this fact. The get_list packet at 11 requires access to both the first argument of the original calling packet and the binding environment. To obtain for a call to the packet at 11 a correctly setup call packet, the pointer context denotes the need for these fields from the parent clause packet and the call packet setup by the calling clause packet. The get_list packet extracts its first argument from the calling packet with an argument selector argsel(2). Its second and third arguments need to be extracted from the binding environment. The packets rooted at 36 and 37 are the routines which simply extract the head and the tail of a two element list respectively. If the guard succeeds the result eventually ripples up to the suspended clause packet and on to the or packet. The computation proceeds nearly identically for the second clause's guard. The packets are rooted at address 9. The guard needs the original calls third field, second argument, and so the pointer context field is different from that of the first clause.

The guard of the third clause is rooted at 12 and the fourth clause at 15. The packets at 12 need to inspect the second field of the call and the packets at 15 the third field of the call; this is realised by the two corresponding pointer contexts. The guards for the third and fourth clauses are both similar to those of the first and second. The difference being that their second conjunct is a get_nil packet so the pointer field to these packets has a pointer context enabling it to obtain the first argument of the call.

The set of body packets for the first and the second clauses are identical as are the body packets for the third and fourth clauses. The first and second clauses' bodies are at address 24. In both of the parent clause packets it suffices to construct a pointer context to 24 which passes the output variable, the third argument in the source Parlog, and the input variable which is not being input matched against a list structure; in the first source Parlog clause this is the the second argument and in the second clause it is the first argument. Thus the calling packet to the body root will consist of a packet whose second field is a reference to the input unmatched variable and third field being a reference to the the output variable.

In order to execute the body conjunction for the first two clauses it is necessary to perform the output match and call merge/3. To do the output match it suffices to perform a put_list and assign, and to do the call, using a put_value packet to load up the new tail variable of the output list. The binding environment of the clause is in the third field of the original ancestor `clause` packet, but the output variable is in the third field of the calling packet. The body requires both the binding environment and the output variable to be present in order for it to execute. The packet at `24` moves the output variable into the fourth field into its copied self. The body calling packet at `25` uses argument selector fields to demand the context information it requires. There is a demand for the binding environment, but because of the field shuffling done by the copy of `24`, it is now not contained in the calling packet. The demand will eventually reach the ancestor `clause` packet and the information will be obtained.

The body packet also needs to create a new binding environment containing the following : a new output variable; the tail of the list bound to the old one; and a temporary variable to hold the result of the list construction before using `assign` to bind the list to the output variable. This is because `assign` is the only primitive which will awaken any tasks suspended on the newly instantiated variable. The fifth field of the packet at `25` contains a reference to the routine at `18` to create a two-element binding list.

The packet at `26` is an `and` constructor packet used to conjoin the three body literal packets. The body packets are held together in a list using the `clause` packet technique. These packets are at `27`, `31`, and `33`. The first body goal to be executed is `put_list`. This is the packet referenced by `27` and is at address `28`. The second and third field of the calling packet to `28` will be set up by the pointer context in the parent at `27`. The eventuality of this is that the second field of the calling packet will contain the input match argument of the source Parlog clause. The third field of the calling packet will be a reference to the two-element binding environment containing the temporary variable, and the new output variable to be used as a tail of the list which will be bound to the old output argument. The third field of the called `put_list` packet will contain a pointer with a pointer context necessary to call a routine to extract the first element of the input match argument in the source Parlog. The second field of the `put_list` packet uses the same routine but a different pointer context is used to pass the third field of the calling packet to it; this is in order to extract the temporary variable. The fourth field of the `put_list` contains a reference to `30` which is a routine to extract the tail of a binding environment, using the pointer context; this is the new output variable. When all of this information is obtained the `put_list` can execute and return a success.

The next literal is given by the `clause` packet at `31`. This is again called in the same context as the previous `clause` packet. It calls the `assign` packet with second field being the original output variable, and third field being a reference to the binding list containing the temporary variable and the new output variable. The second field of the `assign` primitve simply extracts the output variable from the parent call. The third argument calls the routine which will extract the temporary variable thus allowing `assign` to succeed.

The last literal is the tail recursive call to `merge/3`. The `clause` packet is at `33`. The context of the call is set up by the previous `clause` packet. The second field of the call will be the unmatched input argument which is ignored in this logical inference. The third field is the input argument to be matched against a list. The fourth being a reference to the binding environment containing the temporary and the new output variable. The packet at `34` is used to construct the recursive call to the root packet at `1`. The second element of each of the lists in the calling packet contains the new arguments for the recursive call. These are extracted by calling the tail routine at `37` with the appropriate packet using a pointer context. The unmatched input argument is inserted using an argument selector.

The body for the third and fourth clauses is rooted at `35`. It is called from `clause` packets at `4` and `5`. The second field of the calling context packet is the unmatched input variable, the other input variable being matched against `nil` by the guard. Its third field is the output variable. The packet also contains an `assign` primitive to bind the two variables.

Assume the two input lists are of length M and N. It is possible to derive the following statistics. There will be (M + N + 2) calls to the top level root packet at `1`, one for each element of the lists and one for each `nil` element. There will be (M + N) successful guard computations and (M + N) failing guard computations for the guards input matching for a non-empty list. This is because for each succeeding guard, the other guard will be failed, owing to the fact the other has committed. For each of these guard computations, that is (2*(M + N)) of them, there will be an empty-list-matching guard failing. There will be two successful and two failed guards for the matching of the empty lists and four failing non-empty list matching guards. There will be (M + N) successful nonempty list matching clause body calls and two successful calls of the bodies of the empty list matching clauses.

For each call there are 4 parallel reads and four parallel writes to set up the calls to each of the `clause` packets. A non-empty list guard computation, including setting up a binding environment, consists of 26 reads and 22 writes and takes a total of 43 time units, where a time unit is the time taken to read or write a packet to the packet store. An empty list guard computation makes 11 reads and 9 writes and takes 19 time units. A non-empty list body computation, up to the point where the recursive call is set up, takes 42 reads and 51 writes spending 78 time units. For an empty list the body computation would make 6 reads and 5 writes in 10 time units.

As stated in chapter 4 the time unit used is the one reported by GRIP for their packet processing agents access to an IMU. It is perhaps worth noting that GRIP is a hardware prototype and hopefully should therefore give a more realistic measure of the amount of time needed to access a packet store on a physical machine. The time is altered in proportion to the larger packet size here, compared with that of GRIP, and a time unit is 2100 nanoseconds. Below benchmark times for varying numbers of M and N, assuming an infinite number of packet processing elements, are given.

M	N	Time (mS)	LIPS
25	25	13.3	390.2
50	50	26.4	388.7
100	100	52.1	387.9

Table 9. *Timings for* `merge/3` *on the Packet-Rewriting model.*

Appendix 2 A Physical Bit-Level Packet Representation

It is assumed below, and in all simulations, that a 32-bit address space is used.

Packet Type

Currently it is only necessary to support two different types. Therefore 1 bit will suffice.

Suspended Count

This could range from 0 to one less than the number of packets in the packet store in the unlikely event that every other packet ends up in suspended state waiting for the value of a packet. In practice a reasonable limit would be 32 which would mean a total of 5 bits.

Garbage Collection

The content of this field depends upon the type of garbage collection algorithm employed in the system. If a mark-scan method is used than 1 bit will suffice to mark the packet as being a member of a valid subgraph. In the simulator reference counting is used and as in the case of the suspended count 32 would seem to be a reasonable limit on the number of packets that can reference another, so 5 bits are needed.

Packet Context

The packet context consists of set of items, one per major field of the packet. Each item is a member of a set of strictness indicators and can be one of the following: strict, non-strict, fire-once or unused. Each item can be represented in 2 bits and currently in the model only 5 major fields are needed, hence 10 bits will suffice.

Major Fields

There are three types of major field, pointer, argument selector, and value. Therefore, 2 bits are all that is needed to distinguish the type of the field. The contents of a pointer field must hold the address of the packet to which an eventual value can be returned to, together with the context of the pointer. The address space is assumed to be 32 bits. The context denotes which fields of the calling packet are required, along with the demand for the referenced packet. There are 5 major fields so 5 bits are all that are needed. This means that a total of 37 bits for a pointer type field are needed.

An argument selector serves to denote which field of the calling packet is to be inserted *in-situ* into a called packet. As there are 5 major fields, 5 bits are used.

There are 8 types of value field. These are integer, real, character, null, nil, boolean, return address, and function. Thus only 3 bits are needed to distinguish a value field type. Integers are represented in 32 bits. Reals are equivalent to C doubles in the simulator and thus need 64 bits. Characters are represented in 8 bits. There is no requirement for any bits for the contents of null and nil value type fields. A boolean type is either true or false and hence only needs 1 bit. The contents of a return address field have to represent the address of the packet to return to and the number of the appropriate field. The address space is 32 bits and 3 bits suffice to represent a field number. Thus the contents of a return address type value field are 35 bits wide. The function value type field must indicate the particular function to be used and its accompanying argument descriptor. There are currently 52 functions supported, so 6 bits suffice. There are 3 different descriptions of arguments a function can define. These are strict, nonstrict and unused. This means that there will be 2 bits dedicated to each item of which there are 4 so an argument descriptor is 8 bits long. A function value field therefore will be 14 bits wide.

Return Address Field

As in the case for a return address value field it consists of an address and a field number and is therefore 35 bits wide.

The maximum number of bits needed for a major field is to support real numbers. The field here is 64 bits, its type is 2; therefore the largest major field is 66 bits long. Variable sized packets create problems which are outside the scope of this research and are not considered here. As a result the maximum size of a packet 386 bits.

Appendix 3 PPM Instruction Set Listing

Here is the complete set of abstract machine instructions for the PPM abstract machine :

```
add
allocate
assign
data
commit_inh
commit_own
div
environ_inh
environ_own
eq
equal
execute
fail
get_constant
get_list
get_nil
get_structure
halt
less
lesseq
mod
mul
par_proceed
print_term
put_constant
put_list
put_nil
put_structure
```

```
put_value
put_variable
spawn_and_fork
sub
try_committed_or_fork
try_committed_or_fork_else
unify
var
```

Appendix 4 Compiled Form of merge/3 for PPM

The program below is taken from chapter 2 and is used to merge two lists into one.

The chosen program was quicksort of six integers in reverse order, shown below :

```
mode sort(?, ↑).
sort(List, Sorted) ← qsort(List, Sorted, []).

mode qsort(?, ↑, ?).
qsort([U|X], Sortedh, Sortedt) ←
 partition(U, X, X1, X2),
 qsort(X1, Sortedh, [U|Sorted]),
 qsort(X2, Sorted, Sortedt).
qsort([], Sorted, Sorted).

← sort([6, 5, 4, 3, 2, 1]).
```

Here is the corresponding PPM assembly code generated and executed.

```
label(query).
put_constant(1, a1).
put_nil(a0).
put_list(a0, a1, a0).
put_constant(2, a1).
put_list(a0, a1, a0).
put_constant(3, a1).
put_list(a0, a1, a0).
put_constant(4, a1).
put_list(a0, a1, a0).
put_constant(5, a1).
put_list(a0, a1, a0).
put_constant(6, a1).
put_list(a0, a1, a0).
```

```
put_variable(a1).
spawn_and_fork(label('sortpre/2')).
spawn_and_fork(label(print)).
halt.
label(print).
environ_inh.
print_term(a1).
par_proceed.
label('sortpre/2').
environ_inh.
execute(label('sort/2')).
label('sort/2').
put_nil(a2).
execute('qsort/3').
label('qsort/3').
try_committed_or_fork(label(qsort1), label(qsort2)).
par_proceed.
label(qsort1).
environ_own.
allocate(3, 0).
data(a0).
get_list(a0, a0, a3).
commit_own.
put_variable(a4).
put_variable(a5).
put_variable(a6).
spawn_and_fork(label(conj1), label(conj2), label(conj3)).
par_proceed.
label(conj1).
environ_own.
allocate(6, 0).
put_value(a1, a3).
put_value(a2, a4).
```

```
put_value(a3, a5).
execute(label('partition/4')).
label(conj2).
environ_own.
allocate(7, 0).
put_value(a3, a0).
put_value(a0, a4).
put_list(a2, a3, a6).
execute(label('qsort/3')).
label(conj3).
environ_own.
allocate(7, 0).
put_value(a0, a5).
put_value(a1, a6).
execute(label('qsort/3')).
label(qsort2).
environ_inh.
data(a0).
get_nil(a0).
commit_inh.
assign(a1, a2).
par_proceed.
label('partition/4').
try_committed_or_fork(label(clause1), label(clause2), label(clause3)).
par_proceed.
label(clause1).
environ_own.
allocate(4, 0).
data(a0).
data(a1).
get_list(a1, a5, a1).
data(a5).
less(a5, a0).
```

```
commit_own.
put_variable(a7).
put_list(a6, a5, a7).
assign(a2, a6).
put_value(a2, a7).
execute(label('partition/4')).
label(clause2).
environ_own.
allocate(4, 0).
data(a0).
data(a1).
get_list(a1, a5, a1).
data(a5).
lesseq(a0, a5).
commit_own.
put_variable(a7).
put_list(a6, a5, a7).
assign(a3, a6).
put_value(a3, a7).
execute(label('partition/4')).
label(clause3).
environ_inh.
data(a1).
get_nil(a1).
commit_inh.
put_nil(a15).
assign(a2, a15).
assign(a3, a15).
par_proceed.
```

Bibliography

[1] Abe S. & Bandoh T. & Yamaguchi S. & Kurosawa K. & Kiriyama K.
High Performance Integrated Prolog Processor IPP, pp 100-107, Proceedings 14th Annual International Symposium on Computer Architecture, Pittsburgh, Pennsylvania, U.S.A., June 3-6, 1987, also Computer Architecture News, Vol 15, No 2, June 1987

[2] Abe S. & Kiriyama K. & Kurosawa K.-I. & Bandoh T.
Performance Evaluation Of Integrated Prolog Processor IPP, pp 505-510, Proceedings of the International Workshop on Artificial Intelligence for Industrial Applications, Hitachi City, Japan, May 25-27, 1988

[3] Backus J.
Can Programming Be Liberated From The Von-Neumann Style ?, Communications of the ACM, Vol 21, No 8, pp 613-641, August 1978

[4] Banach R.
Formal Specification Of Monstr : Issue 5 - Definitive, Ref. No. FS/MU/RB/019-88, Flagship Project, Department of Computer Science, University of Manhcester, 22nd July 1988

[5] Barendregt H.P.
The Lambda Calculus, Its Syntax and Semantics, North Holland, 1981

[6] Baron U. & Ing B. & Ratcliffe M. & Robert P.
The PEPSys Simulation Project Intermediate Progress Report, Technical Report CA-20, Computer Architecture Group, European Computer-Industry Research Centre GmbH, Munich, West Germany, 8 February 1988

[7] Barklund J. & Hagner N. & Wafin M.
Condition Graphs, pp 435-446, Proceedings of the Fifth International Conference and Symposium on Logic Programming, Seattle, U.S.A., MIT Press, 1988

[8] Bitar P. & Despain A.
Multiprocessor Cache Synchronization Issues, Innovations, Evolution, pp 424-433, Proceedings of the 13th IEEE Annual International Symposium on Computer Architecture, Tokyo, Japan, June 1986

[9] Bloch C.
Source-To-Source Transformations Of Logic Programs, Department of Applied Mathematics, Weizmann Institute of Science, Israel, November 1984

[10] Boulanger A.
Parallelism in the Execution of a Routine Knowledge Rule System on the Butterfly, BBN Laboratories Inc., Report No. 6436, December 1986

[11] Boyer R.S. & Moore J.S.
The Sharing Of Structure In Theorem Proving Programs, pp 101-116, Machine Intelligence, Volume 7, Edinburgh University Press, 1972

[12] British Aerospace Develops The Fastest Artificial Intelligence Computer,
BAe 69/87, British Aerospace News Release, Tuesday, May 12, 1987

[13] Broda K. & Gregory S.
PARLOG For Discrete Event Simulation, Proceedings of the 2nd International Logic Programming Conference, Uppsala, (ed. Tarnlund S.-A.), pp 301-312, July 1984

[14] Burt A.
PARLOG Operating System, PAR 85/3, MSc Thesis, Dept of Computing, Imperial College, September 1985

[15] Butler R. & Lusk E. & McCune W. & Overbeek R.
Parallel Logic Programming For Numerical Applications, pp 375-388, Proceedings of the Third International Conference on Logic Programming, London, United Kingdom, (ed. Shapiro E.), Lecture Notes in Computer Science, Vol 225, Springer Verlag, July 1986

[16] Cardelli L.
Amber, Proceedings of the Treizieme Ecole de Printemps d'Informatique Theorique, Le Val D'Ajol, Vosges, France, May 1985

[17] Carlsson M.
Internals Of Sicstus Prolog Version 0.6, Draft, Logic Programming Systems, SICS, Sweden, August 18 1988

[18] Carlsson M. & Widen J.
SICStus Prolog User's Manual, Research Report R88007, SICS, Sweden, 20 February 1988

[19] Chassin de Kergommeaux J. & Robert P.
An Abstract Machine to Implement Efficiently OR-AND Parallel Prolog, presented at 5th International Conference/Symposium on Logic Programming, Seattle, Washington, U.S.A., August 15-19 1988

[20] Chassin de Kergommeaux J. & Peterson D. & Rapp W. & Westphal H.
The Implementation of PEPSys on an MX-500 Multiprocessor (Intermediate Progress Report), Technical Report CA-38, Computer Architecture Group, European Computer-Industry Research Centre GmbH, Munich, West Germany, 21 March 1988

[21] Chau Y.N.
A PARLOG Expert System Shell, MSc Thesis, Department of Computing, Imperial College, September 1985

[22] Cheese A.B.
A Parallel Model of Inference for Knowledge Bases, Proceedings of the 2nd Alvey Special Interest Group on Knowledge Manipulation Engines (SIGKME) Worksop, Brunel University, May 28-29 1987, also Technical Report TR0001, 5.6.87, Department of Computer Science, University of Nottingham, 1987

[23] Cheese A.B.
Implementing Parlog On Packet-Based Graph Reduction Architectures, Technical Report TR0008, 9.11.87, Department of Computer Science, University of Nottingham, 1987

[24] Cheng C.Y. & Chen C. & Fu H.C.
RPM : A Fast RISC Type Prolog Machine, pp 95-98, Proceedings VLSI and Computers, First International Conference on Computer Technology, Systems and Applications, (COMP EURO 87), Hamburg, May 11-15 1987

[25] Church A.
The Calculi of Lambda-Conversion, Princeton University Press, Princeton, N.J., 1941

[26] Civera P. & Piccinini G. & Zamboni M.
VLSI Architecture For Direct Prolog Language Interpretation, pp 168-172, Proceedings VLSI and Computers, First International Conference on Computer Technology, Systems and Applications (COMP EURO 87), Hamburg, May 11-15 1987

[27] Civera P.L. & Maddaleno F. & Piccini G.L. & Zamboni M.
An Experimental VLSI Prolog Interpreter : Preliminary Measurements and Results, pp 117-126, Proceedings 14th Annual International Symposium on Computer Architecture, Pittsburgh, Pennsylvania, U.S.A., June 3-6, 1987, also Computer Architecture News, Vol 15, No 2, June 1987

[28] Clack C.
Personal Communication, 24 March 1988

[29] Clark K.L. & Tarnlund S.-A.
A First Order Theory of Data and Programs, pp 939-944, Information Processing 77 : Proceedings of the IFIP Congress 77, Elsevier North Holland, Amsterdam, 1977

[30] Clark K.L. & Gregory S.
Notes on Systems Programming in PARLOG, DOC 84/15, Department of Computing, Imperial College, also in Proceedings of the International Conference on Fifth Generation Computer Systems, Tokyo, November 1984, (ed. Aiso H.), Elsevier, North Holland, pp 299-306, July 1984

[31] Clark K. & Gregory S.
Notes on the Implementation of Parlog, Journal of Logic Programming, Vol 2, No 1, pp 17-42, April 1985

[32] Clark K.L. & Foster I.T.
A Declarative Environment for Concurrent Logic Programming, Research Report, Department of Computing, Imperial College, also in Proc. TAPSOFT '87, Pisa, Italy, 1986

[33] Clark K.L. & Gregory S.
Parlog and Prolog United, DOC 87/8, Department of Computing, Imperial College, also 4th International Logic Programming Conference, Melbourne, May 1987

[34] Clocksin W.F. & Mellish C.S.
Programming in Prolog, Second Edition, Springer Verlag, 1984

[35] Codish M. & Shapiro E. Compiling OR-Parallelism Into AND-Parallelism, pp 283-297, Proceedings of the Third International Conference on Logic Programming, London, United Kingdom, July 1986, Lecture Notes in Computer Science Volume 225, Springer Verlag

[36] Connery J.S.
Binding Environments for Parallel Logic Programs in Non-Shared Memory Multiprocessors, pp 457-467, Proceedings 1987 Symposium on Logic Programming, San Francisco, California, U.S.A., August 31 - September 4, 1987

[37] Crammond J.A. & Miller C.D.F.
An Architecture For Parallel Logic Languages, Proceedings of 2nd International Logic Programming Conference, Uppsala, pp 183-194, July 1984

[38] Crammond J.
An Execution Model For Committed-Choice Non-Deterministic Languages, pp 148-158, Proceedings IEEE 1986 Symposium on Logic Programming, Salt Lake City, Utah, U.S.A., September 22-25 1986

[39] Crammond J.
Performance Results for the Execution of Two Different Models of Computation for Parlog, Personal Communication, July 1988

[40] Crammond J.
Implementation of Committed Choice Logic Languages on Shared Memory Multiprocessors, Research Report PAR 88/4 and PhD Thesis, Department of Computing, Imperial College, October 1988

[41] Cripps M.D. & Field A.J. & Reeve M.J.
The Design and Implementation of ALICE : A Parallel Graph Reduction Machine, Department of Computing, Imperial College, in "Functional Programming Languages, Tools and Architectures" (ed. S. Eisenbach), Ellis Horwood, 1986

[42] Darlington J. & Reeve M.
ALICE- A Multi-Processor Reduction Machine for the Parallel Evaluation of Applicative Languages, Proceedings of 1981 ACM Conference on Functional Programming Languages & Computer Architecture

[43] Darlington J. & Reeve M.
ALICE- and the Parallel Evaluation of Logic Programs, Department of Computing, Imperial College, 1983

[44] Darlington J. & Field A.J. & Pull H.
The Unification Of Functional And Logic Languages, in Logic Programming, Functions, Relations, and Equations, pp 37-70, (eds. DeGroot D. & Lindstrom G.), Prentice Hall, 1986

[45] Davidson A.
Objects and Meta Objects in PARLOG, PAR 87/7, Department of Computing, Imperial College, May 1987

[46] Davison A.
Blackboard Systems In PARLOG, Department of Computing, Imperial College, June 1987

[47] Davison A.
POLKA : A PARLOG Object Oriented Language, presented at BCS Parallel Processing and Object Orientated Programming and Systems Specialist Groups Joint One Day Workshop On Parallel And Distributed Object Orientated Programming, School of Oriental and African Studies, University of London, 15th October 1987

[48] Despain A.M.
A High Peformance Hardware Architecture For Design Automation, University of California, Berkeley, U.S.A. and Xenologic Inc, Newark, U.S.A.

[49] Dettmer R.
Flagship A Fifth Generation Machine, IEE Electronics and Power, pp 203-208, March 1986

[50] Dincbas M.
Constraints, Logic Programming And Deductive Databases, pp 1-27, France-Japan Artificial Intelligence and Computer Science Symposium 86, Tokyo Grand Hotel, Japan, 6-8 October 1986

[51] Dincbas M. & Van Hentenryck P. & Simonis H. & Aggoun A. & Graf T. & Berthier F.
The Constraint Logic Programming Language CHIP, pp 693-702, Proceedings of the International Conference on Fifth Generation Computer Systems 1988, Volume 2, Tokyo, Japan, November 28 - December 2 1988

[52] Dobry T.
A High Performance Architecture For Prolog, Report No. UCB/CSD 87/352, Computer Science Division (EECS), University of California, Berkeley, May 1987

[53] Dobry T.
A Coprocessor For AI : LISP, Prolog And Data Bases, Xenologic Inc, Newark, U.S.A.

[54] ECRC
p 2, Logic Programming Newsletter, Vol 2/1, Newsletter of The Association for Logic Programming, July 1988

[55] The Semantics Of Standard ML, LFCS Report Series, ECS-LFCS-87-36, Laboratory for Foundations of Computer Science, Department of Computer Science, University of Edinburgh, August 1987

[56] Ershov A.P.
On The Partial Computation Principle, Information Processing Letters, Vol 6, No 2, pp 38-41, April 1977

[57] Fagin B.S.
A Parallel Execution Model for Prolog, CS Division Report No. UCB/CSD 87/380, Ph.D. Thesis, University of California, Berkeley, U.S.A., November 1987

[58] Fagin B.S. & Despain A.M.
Performance Studies of a Parallel Prolog Architecture, pp 108-116, Proceedings of the 14th IEEE Annual International Symposium on Computer Architecture, Pittsburgh, Pennsylvania, U.S.A., June 2-5 1987

[59] Foster I.T. & Kusalik A. The Logical Treatment of Secondary Storage, pp 58-67, Proceedings IEEE 1986 Symposium on Logic Programming, Salt Lake City, Utah, U.S.A., September 22-25 1986

[60] Foster I.T.
The Compilation of PARLOG For The Sequential PARLOG machine, Dept of Computing, Imperial College, February 1986

[61] Foster I. & Gregory S. & Ringwood G. & Satoh K.
A Sequential Implementation Of Parlog, pp 149-156, Proceedings of the Third International Conference on Logic Programming, London, United Kingdom, (ed. Shapiro E.), Lecture Notes in Computer Science, Vol 225, Springer Verlag, July 1986

[62] Foster I.T.
The PARLOG Programming System (PPS) User Guide/Reference Manual, PAR 87/6, Department of Computing, Imperial College, May 1987

[63] Furukawa K.
Fifth Generation Computer Project : Current Research Activity And Future Plans, TR-228, ICOT Research Center, Tokyo, Japan, January 1986

[64] Futamura Y.
Partial Evaluation Of Computation Process - An Approach To A Compiler-Compiler, Systems, Computers, Control, Vol 2, No 5, pp 721-728, August 1971

[65] Gilbert D.R.
Implementing LOTOS In Parlog, DoC 87/1, Department of Computing, Imperial College, January 1987

[66] Gilbert D.
Executable LOTOS : Using PARLOG To Implement An FDT, PAR 87/3, Department of Computing, Imperial College, May 1987

[67] Glauert J.R.W.
Dactl and its Relationship to Knowledge-Based Systems, Proceedings Of The First Workshop For The Special Interest Group On Knowledge Manipulation Machines (SIGKME), sponsored by the Alvey Directorate, at Reading University, 5th - 6th January, 1987

[68] Glauert J.R.W. & Kennaway J.R. & Sleep M.R.
DACTL : A Computational Model and Compiler Target Language Based on Graph Reduction, Internal Report SYS-C87-03 Declarative Systems Project, University of East Anglia, 10 December 1986

[69] Glauert J.R.W. & Kennaway J.R & Sleep M.R. & Holt N.P. & Reeve M.J. & Watson I.
Specification of Core Dactl 1, Internal Report SYS-C87-09, Declarative Systems Project, University of East Anglia, 26th March 1987

[70] Glauert J.R.W. et. al.
Extensions To Core Dactl1, Declarative Systems Project, University of East Anglia, 1987

[71] Goodman J.
Using Cache Memories to Reduce Processor-Memory Traffic, Proceedings of the 10th IEEE Annual International Symposium on Computer Architecture, Stockholm, Sweden, June 1983

[72] Greenberg M. & Woods V.
Simulating The Flagship Multiprocessor Reduction Machine, Ref. No. FS/MU/MG/027-87, Flagship Project ,Department of Computer Science, University of Manchester, 12th November 1987

[73] Gregory S.
Parallel Logic Programming In Parlog : The Language And Its Implementation, Addison-Wesley Publishers Ltd., 1987

[74] Habata S. & Nakazaki R. & Konagaya A. & Atarashi A. & Umemura M.
Co-Operative High Performance Sequential Inference Machine : CHI, C & C Systems Research Laboratories, NEC Corporation, Kawasaki, Japan, also in Proceedings of ICCD'87, New York, 1987

[75] Hailperin M. & Westphal H.
A Computational Model for PEPSy, Technical Report CA-16, Computer Architecture Group, European Computer-Industry Research Centre GmbH, Munich, West Germany, 21 April 1986

[76] Harper R. & MacQueen D. & Milner R.
Standard ML, LFCS Report Series, ECS-LFCS-86-2, Laboratory for Foundations of Computer Science, University of Edinburgh, March 1986

[77] Herbrand J.
Researches in the Theory of Demonstration, pp 525-581, From Frege to Godel : A Source Book in Mathematical Logic, 1879-1931, Harvard University Press, Mass., 1967

[78] Hirsch M. & Silverman W. & Shapiro E.
Layers of Protection and Control in the Logix System, CS86-19, Department of Computer Science, Weizmann Institute of Science, Israel, December 1985, Revised June 1986

[79] Hoare C.A.R.
Quicksort, pp 10-15, Computer Journal, Volume 5, Number 1, 1962

[80] Hoare C.A.R.
Communicating Sequential Processes, Communications of the ACM, Vol 21, No 8, pp 666-677, August 1978

[81] IPSC System Product Summary, Intel Scientific Computers, Beaverton, Oregon, U.S.A

[82] Jaffar J. & Lassez J.-L.
Constraint Logic Programming, pp 111-119, Conference Record of the Fourteenth Annual ACM Symposium on Principles of Programming Languages, Munich, West Germany, Jan 1987

[83] Kahn K.M.
Partial Evaluation As An Example Of The Relationships Between Programming Methodology And Artificial Intelligence, UPMAIL Technical Report No. 23, Uppsala Programming Methodology and Artificial Intelligence Laboratory, Uppsala University, Computing Science Department, Uppsala, Sweden, October 15 1983

[84] Kahn K. & Tribble E.D. & Miller M.S. & Bobrow D.G.
Vulcan : Logical Concurrent Objects, Knowledge Systems Area, Intelligent System Laboratory, Xerox Palo Alto Research Center, 1986

[85] Kahn K. & Bobrow D.G. & Miller M.S.
Objects in Concurrent Logic Programming Languages, Knowledge Systems Area, Intelligent System Laboratory, Xerox Palo Alto Research Center, April 1986

[86] Kahn K.M. & Abbott C. & Bobrow D.G. & Miller M.S. & Tribble E.D.
Concurrent Logic Programming Abstractions, pp 141-162, Proceedings 1988 Spring Symposium Series, Parallel Models Of Intelligence : How Can Slow Components Think So Fast ?, Stanford University, March 22-24 1988

[87] Kahn K.M. & Miller M.S.
Language Design And Open Systems, pp 291-313, The Ecology Of Computation, (ed. Huberman B.A.), Elsevier Science Publishers B.V. (North Holland),1988

[88] Kimura Y. & Chikayama T.
An Abstract KL1 Machine And Its Instruction Set, pp 468-477, Proceedings 1987 Symposium on Logic Programming, San Francisco, U.S.A., August 31 - September 4 1987

[89] Kishi M. & Kuno E. & Rokusawa K. & Ito N.
The Dataflow-Based Parallel Inference Machine To Support Two Basic Languages In KL1, TR-114, ICOT Research Center, Tokyo, Japan, July 1985

[90] Kishimoto M. & Hosoi A. & Kumon K. & Hattori A.
An Evaluation Of The FGHC Via Practical Application Programs, pp 516-525, Proceedings 1987 Symposium on Logic Programming, San Francisco, U.S.A., August 31 - September 4 1987

[91] Kishishita M. & Tanaka J. & Miyazaki T. & Taki K. & Chikayama T.
Distributed Implementation of FGHC : Towards The Realization Of Multi-PSI System, TR-159, ICOT Research Center, Tokyo, Japan, March 1986

[92] Komorowski H.J.
Partial Evaluation As A Means For Inferencing Data Structures In An Applicative Language : A Theory And Implementation In The Case Of Prolog, 9th ACM Principles of Programming Languages, pp 255-267, 1982

[93] Konagaya A. & Nakazaki R.
A Co-Operative Programming Environment For A Back-End Type Sequential Inference Machine CHI, C & C Systems Research Laboratories, NEC Corporation, Kawasaki, Japan, March 16 1987

[94] Kuno E. & Ito N. & Sato M. & Rokusawa K.
The Architecture And Preliminary Results Of The Experimental Parallel Inference Machine PIM-D, TR-160, ICOT Research Center, Tokyo, Japan, March 1986

[95] Lam M. & Gregory S.
PARLOG and ALICE : A Marriage of Convenience, DOC 87/7, Department of Computing, Imperial College, March 1987, also at 4th International Logic Programming Conference, Melbourne, May 1987

[96] Lam M. & Gregory S.
Implementation Of Parlog On Dactl, Department of Computing, Imperial College, March 7 1988

[97] Landin P.J.
The Mechanical Evaluation Of Expressions, Computer Journal, Vol 6, No 4, pp 308-320, 1963

[98] Levy J.
A Unification Algorithm for Concurrent Prolog, Proceedings of 2nd International Logic Programming Conference (ed. Tarnlund S.-A.), Uppsala University, Uppsala, Sweden pp 333-341, July 2-6 1984

[99] Lloyd J.W.
Foundations of Logic Programming, Symbolic Computation Series, Springer Verlag, 1984

[100] Mierowsky C. & Taylor S. & Shapiro E. & Levy J. & Safra M.
The Design and Implementation of Flat Concurrent Prolog, CS85-09, Department of Applied Mathematics, Weizmann Institute of Science, Israel, July 1985

[101] Mills J.W.
Coming to Grips with a RISC : A Report of the Progress of the LOW RISC Design Group, pp 53-62, Computer Architecture News, Vol 15, No 1, March 1987

[102] Nakashima H. et. al.
Evaluation Of PSI Micro-Interpreter, TR-142, ICOT Research Center, November 1985

[103] Nakashima H. & Nakajima K.
Hardware Architecture of the Sequential Inference Machine PSI-II, pp 104-113, Proceedings 1987 IEEE Symposium on Logic Programming, San Francisco, U.S.A., August 31 - September 4 1987

[104] Nakazaki R. et. al.
Design of a High-Speed Prolog Machine (HPM), TM-0105, ICOT Research Center, Tokyo, Japan, April 1985

[105] Neumann P.G.
Some Computer-Related Disasters And Other Egregious Horrors, ACM SIGSOFT Software Engineering Notes, Vol 10, No 1, 1985

[106] Nguyen T.M. & Srini V.P. & Despain A.M.
A Two-Tier Memory Architecture for High-Performance Multiprocessor Systems, pp 326-336, Proceedings of the 1988 International Conference on Supercomputing, St. Malo, France, July 4-8, 1988, ACM Press 1988

[107] Nilsson & Tanaka H.
- FLENG Prolog - The Language Which Turns Supercomputers Into Parallel Prolog Machines, pp 170-179, Logic Programming '86, Proceedings of the 5th Conference, Tokyo, Japan, Lecture Notes in Computer Science Volume 264, Springer-Verlag, June 86

[108] Nilsson M. & Tanaka H.
Massively Parallel Implementation of Flat GHC on the Connection Machine, pp 1031-1040, Proceedings of the International Conference on Fifth Generation Computer Systems, Tokyo, 1988

[109] Nishikawa H. & Yokota M. & Yamamoto A. & Taki K. & Uchida S.
The Personal Inference Machine (PSI) : Its design Philosophy and Machine Architecture, TR-013, ICOT Research Center, Tokyo, Japan, June 1983, also in Proceedings of Logic Programming Workshop, Portugal 1983

[110] Noye J. & Syre J.-C. et al.
ICM3 : Design And Evaluation Of An Inference Crunching Machine, pp 1-13, Proceedings of 5th International Workshop on Databse Machines, Mampei Hotel, Karuizawa, Japan, October 5-9 1987

[111] O'Donnell J.T.
A Massively Parallel Architecture For Applicative Programming, Seminar at University of Manchester, 28 June 1988

[112] Oldfield J.V. & Stormon C.D. & Brule M.
The Application of VLSI Content-Addressable Memories to the Acceleration of Logic Programming Systems, pp 27-30, Proceedings VLSI and Computers, First International Conference on Computer Technology, Systems and Applications, (COMP EURO 87), Hamburg May 11-15 1987

[113] Papadopoulos G.
PARLOG84 -> DACTL0, Personal Communication, 13 May 1986

[114] Papadopoulos G.A. & Glauert J.R.W.
Towards A Common Implementation For Parallel Logic Languages Based On An Intermediate Compiler Target Language, Proceedings of the Second Workshop for the Special Interest Group on Knowledge Manipulation Engines (SIGKME), Brunel University, 28-29 May 1987

[115] Papadopoulos G.A.
A High-Level Parallel Implementation Of PARLOG, Internal Report SYS-C88-05, Declarative Systems Project, University of East Anglia, March 1988

[116] Perry N.
Hope +, IC/FPR/LANG/2.5.1/7, Issue 3, Department of Computing, Imperial College, March 1987

[117] Peyton Jones S. L. & Clack C. & Salkild J. & Hardie M.
GRIP - A High Peformance Architecture for Parallel Graph Reduction, Proceedings IFIP Conference on Functional Programming Languages and Computer Architecture, Portland, USA, pp 98-112, Springer Verlag Lecture Notes in Computer Science no. 274 (ed. Kahn G.), September 1987

[118] Peyton Jones S. L.
Personal Communication, 11 March 1988

[119] Proctor B.J.
Next Generation Computer Systems, pp 809-814, Proceedings VLSI and Computers, First International Conference on Computer Technology, Systems and Applications (COMP EURO 87), Hamburg, May 11-15 1987

[120] Pudner A.
DLM - A Powerful AI Computer For Embedded Expert Systems, British Aerospace, Naval And Electronic Systems Division, Berkshire, UK

[121] Quintus Prolog Reference Manual Version 10, Quintus Computer Systems, Inc, Mountain View, California, U.S.A., February 1987

[122] Profiles In Prolog, BEACON : A Configurator For Unisys Hardware Systems, in ?-consult(user)., The Quintus Newsletter, pp 3-4, Quintus Computer Systems, Inc., Mountain View, California, U.S.A., June 1987

[123] Quintus Prolog In The Nuclear Industry, Quintus Computer Systems, Inc., Mountain View, California, U.S.A.

[124] Quintus Prolog In Cargo Loading, Quintus Computer Systems, Inc., Mountain View, California, U.S.A.

[125] Quintus Prolog In Aerospace, Quintus Computer Systems, Inc., Mountain View, California, U.S.A.

[126] Reeve M.
The ALICE Compiler Target Language, Department of Computing, Imperial College, May 1981

[127] Reeve M.
An Introduction to the ALICE Compiler Target Language, Department of Computing, Imperial College, July 1981

[128] Reeve M.
A BNF Description Of The Alice Compiler Target Language, Department of Computing, Imperial College, 1985

[129] Ribler R.L.
The Integration Of The Xenologic X-1 Artificial Intelligence Coprocessor With General Purpose Computers, Xenologic Inc, Newark, U.S.A.

[130] Robinson J.A.
A Machine-Oriented Logic Based On The Resolution Principle, pp 23-41, Journal of the ACM, Vol 12, No 1, January 1965

[131] Robinson I.
A Prolog Processor Based On A Pattern Matching Memory Device, pp 172-179, Third International Conference on Logic Programming, London 1986

[132] Roussel P.
Prolog : Manuel De Reference Et D'Utilisation, Groupe d'Intelligence Artificielle, Universite d'Aix-Marseille, Luminy, France, 1975

[133] Safra S. & Shapiro E.
Meta Interpreters for Real, CS86-11, Department of Computer Science, Weizmann Institute of Science, Israel, May 1986

[134] Saraswat V.A.
Concurrent Logic Programming Languages, Thesis Proposal, 1 November 1985

[135] Saraswat V.A.
Problems With Concurrent Prolog, CMU-CS-86-100, Department of Computer Science, Carnegie-Mellon University, May 1985, revised January 1986

[136] Saraswat V.A.
The Concurrent Logic Programming Language CP : Definition And Operational Semantics (Extended Abstract), pp 49-62, Conference Record of the Fourteenth Annual ACM Symposium on Principles of Programming Languages, Munich, West Germany, 21-23 Jan 1987

[137] Sargeant J.
Load Balancing, Locality and Parallelism Control in Fine-Grain Parallel Machines, UMCS-86-11-5, Department of Computer Science, University of Manchester, 12 January 1987

[138] Sato M. & Shimizu H. & Matsumoto A. & Rokusawa K. & Goto A.
KL1 Execution Model For PIM Cluster With Shared Memory, TR-250, ICOT Research Center, Tokyo, Japan, April 1987

[139] Seo K. & Yokota T.
Pegasus : A Risc Processor For High-Performance Execution Of Prolog Programs, VLSI '87, pp 261-274, North Holland, 1988

[140] Balance Technical Summary, Sequent Computer Systems, Inc., Man-0110-00, November 19 1986

[141] Shankar S.
A Hierarchical Associative Memory Architecture For Logic Programming Unification, presented at Fifth International Conference/Symposium on Logic Programming, Seattle, Washington, August 15-19 1988

[142] Shapiro E.Y.
A Subset Concurrent Prolog and its Interpreter, TR-003, ICOT Research Center, Tokyo, Japan, January 1983

[143] Shapiro E.
Concurrent Prolog : A Progress Report, IEEE Computer, Vol 19, No 8, pp 44-58, August 1986

[144] Shen K.
An Investigation of the Argonne Model of Or-Parallel Prolog, UMCS-87-1-1, Department of Computer Science, University of Manchester, November 1986

[145] Shobatake Y. & Aiso H.
A Unification Processor Based on a Uniformly Structured Cellular Hardware, pp 140-148, 13th Annual International Symposium on Computer Architecture, Tokyo, Japan, 1986

[146] Short B.K.
Use of Instruction Set Simulators to Evaluate the LOW RISC, pp 63-67, Computer Architecture News, Vol 15, No 1, March 1987

[147] Silverman W. & Hirsch M. & Houri A. & Shapiro E.
The Logix System User Manual Version 1.21, CS-21, Department of Computer Science, Weizmann Insitute of Science, Rehovot, Israel, 1986

[148] Smith K.
Britain Makes Major Bid To Build Commercial Fifth-Generation Machine, Electronics, pp 26-27, July 8 1985

[149] Srini V.P. et. al.
VLSI Implementation Of A Prolog Processor, University of California, Berkeley, U.S.A.

[150] Storman C.D. & Brule M.R. & Oldfield J.V. & Ribeiro J.C.D.F.
An Architecture Based on Content-Addressable Memory for the Rapid Execution of Prolog, presented at Fifth International Conference/Symposium on Logic Programming, Seattle, Washington, August 15-19 1988

[151] Syre J.-C.
Presentation, Department of Computer Science, University of Manchester, 1985

[152] Syre J.-C.
Prolog Machines, news item posted to Usenet, October 1987

[153] Takeuchi A. & Furukawa K.
Parallel Logic Programming Languages, pp 242-254, Proceedings of the Third International Conference on Logic Programming, London, United Kingdom, July 1986, Lecture Notes in Computer Science Volume 225, Springer Verlag

[154] Taki K. et. al.
Hardware Design and Implementation of the Personal Sequential Inference Machine (PSI), TR-075, ICOT Research Center, Tokyo, Japan, August 1984, also in Proceedings of FGCS 84, Tokyo, 1984

[155] Taki K.
The Parallel Software Research And Development Tool : Multi-PSI System, TR-237, ICOT Research Center, Tokyo, Japan, March 1987

[156] Taki K. & Nakajima K. & Nakashima H. & Ikeda M.
Performance And Architecture Evaluation Of The PSI Machine, pp 128-135, Proceedings of the Second International Conference on Architectural Support for Programming Languages and Operating Systems, (ASPLOS II), Palo Alto, California, U.S.A., October 5-8 1987

[157] Tanaka J. et. al.
Guarded Horn Clauses And Experiences With Parallel Logic Programming, TR-168, ICOT Research Center, Tokyo, Japan, April 1986

[158] Tarnlund S.-A.
Test Of An Inference System For Parallel Logic Programming, p 7, Logic Programming Newsletter, Vol 2/1, Newsletter for The Association for Logic Programming, July 1988

[159] Taylor S. & Av-Ron E. & Shapiro E.
A Layered Method for Process and Code Mapping, CS86-17, Department of Applied Mathematics, Weizmann Institute of Science, Israel, March 25th 1986

[160] Taylor H.
PARLOG All Solutions Server, Technical Report No. 87/2, Computer Science Department, Heriot-Watt University, April 1987

[161] Taylor H.
And-Parallel Kernel PARLOG - A Lingua Franca For Emulating GHC And PARLOG, Technical Report No. 87/08, Computer Science Department, Heriot-Watt University, November 1987

[162] Taylor H. & Williams M.H.
Implementing Parlog For Database Applications, Technical Report No. 87/10, Computer Science Department, Heriot-Watt University, 1987

[163] Taylor H.
Kelpie - An And-Parallel Kernel Parlog Emulator, Technical Report No. 87/11, Computer Science Department, Heriot-Watt University, December 1987

[164] Tick E.
An Overlapped Prolog Processor, Technical Note 308, SRI International, October 1983

[165] Tinker P.
Fast Memory Mapping To Use All Memory On The BBN Butterfly Parallel Processor, Computer Science Department, University of Utah, 13 January 1987

[166] Trehan R. & Wilk P.F.
A Parallel Chart Parser For The Committed Choice Non-Deterministic Logic Languages, pp 212-232, Proceedings of the Fifth International Conference and Symposium on Logic Programming, Seattle, U.S.A., MIT Press, 1988

[167] Turner D.A.
Miranda : A Non-Strict Functional Language With Polymorphic Types, Functional Programming Languages and Computer Architecture, Proceedings, Nancy, France, Lecture Notes in Computer Science, Vol 201, pp 1-16 Springer Verlag, September 1985

[168] Uchida S. & Yokota M. & Yamamoto A. & Taki K. & Nishikawa H.
Outline of the Personal Sequential Inference Machine : PSI, TM-0005, ICOT Research Center, Tokyo, Japan, April 1983, also in New Generation Computing, Vol 1, No 1, 1983

[169] Ueda K.
Concurrent Prolog Re-examined, TR-102, ICOT Research Center, Tokyo, November 1985

[170] Ueda K.
Guarded Horn Clauses, Thesis submitted to the Information Engineering Course of the University of Tokyo, Graduate School in partial fulfillment of the Requirements for the Degree of Doctor of Engineering, March 1986

[171] Wadler P.L.
Posting to fp Bulletin Board, 2nd August 1988

[172] Wadsworth C.P. Semantics and Pragmatics of The Lambda Calculus, D.Phil Thesis, University of Oxford, 1971

[173] Wallace M. Negation By Constraints: A Sound And Efficient Implementation Of Negation In Deductive Databases, pp 253-263, Proceedings 1987 Symposium on Logic Programming, San Francisco, U.S.A., August 31 - September 4 1987

[174] Warren D.H.D.
Applied Logic - Its Use And Implementation As A Programming Tool, Technical Note 290, SRI International, June 1983

[175] Warren D.H.D.
An Abstract Prolog Instruction set, Technical Note 309, SRI International, 31 August 1983

[176] Warren D.H.D.
Logic Programming After Alvey - Position Paper, Department of Computer Science, University of Manchester, 1987

[177] Watson Ian & Watson Paul & Woods Viv
Parallel Data-Driven Graph Reduction, Document, Dept. of Computer Science, Univ. of Manchester, IFIP TC-10 Working Conference on Fifth Generation Computer Architecture, UMIST, Manchester, July 15-18 1985

[178] Watson P. & Watson I.
Evaluating Functional Programs On The Flagship Machine, Department of Computer Science, University of Manchester, February 16 1987

[179] Watson I. & Woods V. & Watson P. & Banach R. & Greenberg M. & Sargeant J.
Flagship : A Parallel Architecture For Declarative Programming, Issue No. 2, Ref. No. FS/MU/IW/006-88, Flagship Project, Department of Computer Science, University of Manchester, 29th March 1988

[180] Westphal H. & Robert P. & Chassin J. & Syre J.-C.
The PEPSys Model : Combining Backtracking, AND- and OR-Parallelism, Proceedings 4th Symposium on Logic Programming, pp 436-448, September 1987

[181] Wilk P. & Trehan R.
Committed Choice Non-Deterministic Logic Languages For Ai Problem Solving, Logic Programming and Reduction Workshop, York, England, 14th, 15th December 1987

[182] Winston P.H. & Horn B.K.P.
Lisp, Addison Wesley Publishing Company, 1984

[183] Yamaguchi S. & Bandoh T. & Kurosawa K. & Morioka M.
Architecture Of High Performance Integrated Prolog Processor IPP, 1987 Fall Joint Computer Conference, Dallas, Texas

[184] Yang R. & Aiso H.
P-Prolog : A Parallel Logic Language Based On Exclusive Relation, pp 255-269, Proceedings of the Third International Conference on Logic Programming, London, United Kingdom, (ed. Shapiro E.), Lecture Notes in Computer Science, Vol 225, Springer Verlag, July 1986

[185] Yang R.
P-Prolog : A Parallel Logic Programming Language, Series in Computer Science - Vol. 9, World Scientific Publishing Co. Ltd., 1987

[186] Yokota M. & Yamamoto A. & Taki K. & Nishikawa H. & Uchida S.
The Design and Implementation of a Personal Sequential Inference Machine: PSI, TR-045, ICOT Research Center, Tokyo, Japan, February 1984, also in New Generation Computing, Vol 1, No 2, 1984

Lecture Notes in Computer Science

For information about Vols. 1–529
please contact your bookseller or Springer-Verlag

Vol. 530: D. H. Pitt, P.-L. Curien, S. Abramsky, A. M. Pitts, A. Poigné, D. E. Rydeheard (Eds.), Category Theory and Computer Science. Proceedings, 1991. VII, 301 pages. 1991.

Vol. 531: E. M. Clarke, R. P. Kurshan (Eds.), Computer-Aided Verification. Proceedings, 1990. XIII, 372 pages. 1991.

Vol. 532: H. Ehrig, H.-J. Kreowski, G. Rozenberg (Eds.), Graph Grammars and Their Application to Computer Science. Proceedings, 1990. X, 703 pages. 1991.

Vol. 533: E. Börger, H. Kleine Büning, M. M. Richter, W. Schönfeld (Eds.), Computer Science Logic. Proceedings, 1990. VIII, 399 pages. 1991.

Vol. 534: H. Ehrig, K. P. Jantke, F. Orejas, H. Reichel (Eds.), Recent Trends in Data Type Specification. Proceedings, 1990. VIII, 379 pages. 1991.

Vol. 535: P. Jorrand, J. Kelemen (Eds.), Fundamentals of Artificial Intelligence Research. Proceedings, 1991. VIII, 255 pages. 1991. (Subseries LNAI).

Vol. 536: J. E. Tomayko, Software Engineering Education. Proceedings, 1991. VIII, 296 pages. 1991.

Vol. 537: A. J. Menezes, S. A. Vanstone (Eds.), Advances in Cryptology – CRYPTO '90. Proceedings. XIII, 644 pages. 1991.

Vol. 538: M. Kojima, N. Megiddo, T. Noma, A. Yoshise, A Unified Approach to Interior Point Algorithms for Linear Complementarity Problems. VIII, 108 pages. 1991.

Vol. 539: H. F. Mattson, T. Mora, T. R. N. Rao (Eds.), Applied Algebra, Algebraic Algorithms and Error-Correcting Codes. Proceedings, 1991. XI, 489 pages. 1991.

Vol. 540: A. Prieto (Ed.), Artificial Neural Networks. Proceedings, 1991. XIII, 476 pages. 1991.

Vol. 541: P. Barahona, L. Moniz Pereira, A. Porto (Eds.), EPIA '91. Proceedings, 1991. VIII, 292 pages. 1991. (Subseries LNAI).

Vol. 542: Z. W. Ras, M. Zemankova (Eds.), Methodologies for Intelligent Systems. Proceedings, 1991. X, 644 pages. 1991. (Subseries LNAI).

Vol. 543: J. Dix, K. P. Jantke, P. H. Schmitt (Eds.), Nonmonotonic and Inductive Logic. Proceedings, 1990. X, 243 pages. 1991. (Subseries LNAI).

Vol. 544: M. Broy, M. Wirsing (Eds.), Methods of Programming. XII, 268 pages. 1991.

Vol. 545: H. Alblas, B. Melichar (Eds.), Attribute Grammars, Applications and Systems. Proceedings, 1991. IX, 513 pages. 1991.

Vol. 546: O. Herzog, C.-R. Rollinger (Eds.), Text Understanding in LILOG. XI, 738 pages. 1991. (Subseries LNAI).

Vol. 547: D. W. Davies (Ed.), Advances in Cryptology – EUROCRYPT '91. Proceedings, 1991. XII, 556 pages. 1991.

Vol. 548: R. Kruse, P. Siegel (Eds.), Symbolic and Quantitative Approaches to Uncertainty. Proceedings, 1991. XI, 362 pages. 1991.

Vol. 549: E. Ardizzone, S. Gaglio, F. Sorbello (Eds.), Trends in Artificial Intelligence. Proceedings, 1991. XIV, 479 pages. 1991. (Subseries LNAI).

Vol. 550: A. van Lamsweerde, A. Fugetta (Eds.), ESEC '91. Proceedings, 1991. XII, 515 pages. 1991.

Vol. 551:S. Prehn, W. J. Toetenel (Eds.), VDM '91. Formal Software Development Methods. Volume 1. Proceedings, 1991. XIII, 699 pages. 1991.

Vol. 552: S. Prehn, W. J. Toetenel (Eds.), VDM '91. Formal Software Development Methods. Volume 2. Proceedings, 1991. XIV, 430 pages. 1991.

Vol. 553: H. Bieri, H. Noltemeier (Eds.), Computational Geometry - Methods, Algorithms and Applications '91. Proceedings, 1991. VIII, 320 pages. 1991.

Vol. 554: G. Grahne, The Problem of Incomplete Information in Relational Databases. VIII, 156 pages. 1991.

Vol. 555: H. Maurer (Ed.), New Results and New Trends in Computer Science. Proceedings, 1991. VIII, 403 pages. 1991.

Vol. 556: J.-M. Jacquet, Conclog: A Methodological Approach to Concurrent Logic Programming. XII, 781 pages. 1991.

Vol. 557: W. L. Hsu, R. C. T. Lee (Eds.), ISA '91 Algorithms. Proceedings, 1991. X, 396 pages. 1991.

Vol. 558: J. Hooman, Specification and Compositional Verification of Real-Time Systems. VIII, 235 pages. 1991.

Vol. 559: G. Butler, Fundamental Algorithms for Permutation Groups. XII, 238 pages. 1991.

Vol. 560: S. Biswas, K. V. Nori (Eds.), Foundations of Software Technology and Theoretical Computer Science. Proceedings, 1991. X, 420 pages. 1991.

Vol. 561: C. Ding, G. Xiao, W. Shan, The Stability Theory of Stream Ciphers. IX, 187 pages. 1991.

Vol. 562: R. Breu, Algebraic Specification Techniques in Object Oriented Programming Environments. XI, 228 pages. 1991.

Vol. 563: A. Karshmer, J. Nehmer (Eds.), Operating Systems of the 90s and Beyond. Proceedings, 1991. X, 285 pages. 1991.

Vol. 564: I. Herman, The Use of Projective Geometry in Computer Graphics. VIII, 146 pages. 1992.

Vol. 565: J. D. Becker, I. Eisele, F. W. Mündemann (Eds.), Parallelism, Learning, Evolution. Proceedings, 1989. VIII, 525 pages. 1991. (Subseries LNAI).

Vol. 566: C. Delobel, M. Kifer, Y. Masunaga (Eds.), Deductive and Object-Oriented Databases. Proceedings, 1991. XV, 581 pages. 1991.

Vol. 567: H. Boley, M. M. Richter (Eds.), Processing Declarative Kowledge. Proceedings, 1991. XII, 427 pages. 1991. (Subseries LNAI).

Vol. 568: H.-J. Bürckert, A Resolution Principle for a Logic with Restricted Quantifiers. X, 116 pages. 1991. (Subseries LNAI).

Vol. 569: A. Beaumont, G. Gupta (Eds.), Parallel Execution of Logic Programs. Proceedings, 1991. VII, 195 pages. 1991.

Vol. 570: R. Berghammer, G. Schmidt (Eds.), Graph-Theoretic Concepts in Computer Science. Proceedings, 1991. VIII, 253 pages. 1992.

Vol. 571: J. Vytopil (Ed.), Formal Techniques in Real-Time and Fault-Tolerant Systems. Proceedings, 1992. IX, 620 pages. 1991.

Vol. 572: K. U. Schulz (Ed.), Word Equations and Related Topics. Proceedings, 1990. VII, 256 pages. 1992.

Vol. 573: G. Cohen, S. N. Litsyn, A. Lobstein, G. Zémor (Eds.), Algebraic Coding. Proceedings, 1991. X, 158 pages. 1992.

Vol. 574: J. P. Banâtre, D. Le Métayer (Eds.), Research Directions in High-Level Parallel Programming Languages. Proceedings, 1991. VIII, 387 pages. 1992.

Vol. 575: K. G. Larsen, A. Skou (Eds.), Computer Aided Verification. Proceedings, 1991. X, 487 pages. 1992.

Vol. 576: J. Feigenbaum (Ed.), Advances in Cryptology - CRYPTO '91. Proceedings. X, 485 pages. 1992.

Vol. 577: A. Finkel, M. Jantzen (Eds.), STACS 92. Proceedings, 1992. XIV, 621 pages. 1992.

Vol. 578: Th. Beth, M. Frisch, G. J. Simmons (Eds.), Public-Key Cryptography: State of the Art and Future Directions. XI, 97 pages. 1992.

Vol. 579: S. Toueg, P. G. Spirakis, L. Kirousis (Eds.), Distributed Algorithms. Proceedings, 1991. X, 319 pages. 1992.

Vol. 580: A. Pirotte, C. Delobel, G. Gottlob (Eds.), Advances in Database Technology – EDBT '92. Proceedings. XII, 551 pages. 1992.

Vol. 581: J.-C. Raoult (Ed.), CAAP '92. Proceedings. VIII, 361 pages. 1992.

Vol. 582: B. Krieg-Brückner (Ed.), ESOP '92. Proceedings. VIII, 491 pages. 1992.

Vol. 583: I. Simon (Ed.), LATIN '92. Proceedings. IX, 545 pages. 1992.

Vol. 584: R. E. Zippel (Ed.), Computer Algebra and Parallelism. Proceedings, 1990. IX, 114 pages. 1992.

Vol. 585: F. Pichler, R. Moreno Díaz (Eds.), Computer Aided System Theory – EUROCAST '91. Proceedings. X, 761 pages. 1992.

Vol. 586: A. Cheese, Parallel Execution of Parlog. IX, 184 pages. 1992.

Vol. 587: R. Dale, E. Hovy, D. Rösner, O. Stock (Eds.), Aspects of Automated Natural Language Generation. Proceedings, 1992. VIII, 311 pages. 1992. (Subseries LNAI).

Vol. 588: G. Sandini (Ed.), Computer Vision – ECCV '92. Proceedings. XV, 909 pages. 1992.

Vol. 589: U. Banerjee, D. Gelernter, A. Nicolau, D. Padua (Eds.), Languages and Compilers for Parallel Computing. Proceedings, 1991. IX, 419 pages. 1992.

Vol. 590: B. Fronhöfer, G. Wrightson (Eds.), Parallelization in Inference Systems. Proceedings, 1990. VIII, 372 pages. 1992. (Subseries LNAI).

Vol. 591: H. P. Zima (Ed.), Parallel Computation. Proceedings, 1991. IX, 451 pages. 1992.

Vol. 592: A. Voronkov (Ed.), Logic Programming. Proceedings, 1991. IX, 514 pages. 1992. (Subseries LNAI).

Vol. 593: P. Loucopoulos (Ed.), Advanced Information Systems Engineering. Proceedings. XI, 650 pages. 1992.

Vol. 594: B. Monien, Th. Ottmann (Eds.), Data Structures and Efficient Algorithms. VIII, 389 pages. 1992.

Vol. 595: M. Levene, The Nested Universal Relation Database Model. X, 177 pages. 1992.

Vol. 596: L.-H. Eriksson, L. Hallnäs, P. Schroeder-Heister (Eds.), Extensions of Logic Programming. Proceedings, 1991. VII, 369 pages. 1992. (Subseries LNAI).

Vol. 597: H. W. Guesgen, J. Hertzberg, A Perspective of Constraint-Based Reasoning. VIII, 123 pages. 1992. (Subseries LNAI).

Vol. 598: S. Brookes, M. Main, A. Melton, M. Mislove, D. Schmidt (Eds.), Mathematical Foundations of Programming Semantics. Proceedings, 1991. VIII, 506 pages. 1992.

Vol. 599: Th. Wetter, K.-D. Althoff, J. Boose, B. R. Gaines, M. Linster, F. Schmalhofer (Eds.), Current Developments in Knowledge Acquisition - EKAW '92. Proceedings. XIII, 444 pages. 1992. (Subseries LNAI).

Vol. 600: J. W. de Bakker, K. Huizing, W. P. de Roever, G. Rozenberg (Eds.), Real-Time: Theory in Practice. Proceedings, 1991. VIII, 723 pages. 1992.

Vol. 601: D. Dolev, Z. Galil, M. Rodeh (Eds.), Theory of Computing and Systems. Proceedings, 1992. VIII, 220 pages. 1992.

Vol. 602: I. Tomek (Ed.), Computer Assisted Learning. Proceedigs, 1992. X, 615 pages. 1992.

Vol. 603: J. van Katwijk (Ed.), Ada: Moving Towards 2000. Proceedings, 1992. VIII, 324 pages. 1992.

Vol. 604: F. Belli, F.-J. Radermacher (Eds.), Industrial and Engineering Applications of Artificial Intelligence and Expert Systems. Proceedings, 1992. XV, 702 pages. 1992. (Subseries LNAI).

Vol. 605: D. Etiemble, J.-C. Syre (Eds.), PARLE '92. Parallel Architectures and Languages Europe. Proceedings, 1992. XVII, 984 pages. 1992.

Vol. 607: D. Kapur (Ed.), Automated Deduction – CADE-11. Proceedings, 1992. XV, 793 pages. 1992. (Subseries LNAI).

Vol. 608: C. Frasson, G. Gauthier, G. I. McCalla (Eds.), Intelligent Tutoring Systems. Proceedings, 1992. XIV, 686 pages. 1992.